Ocean Coloring Books for Adults

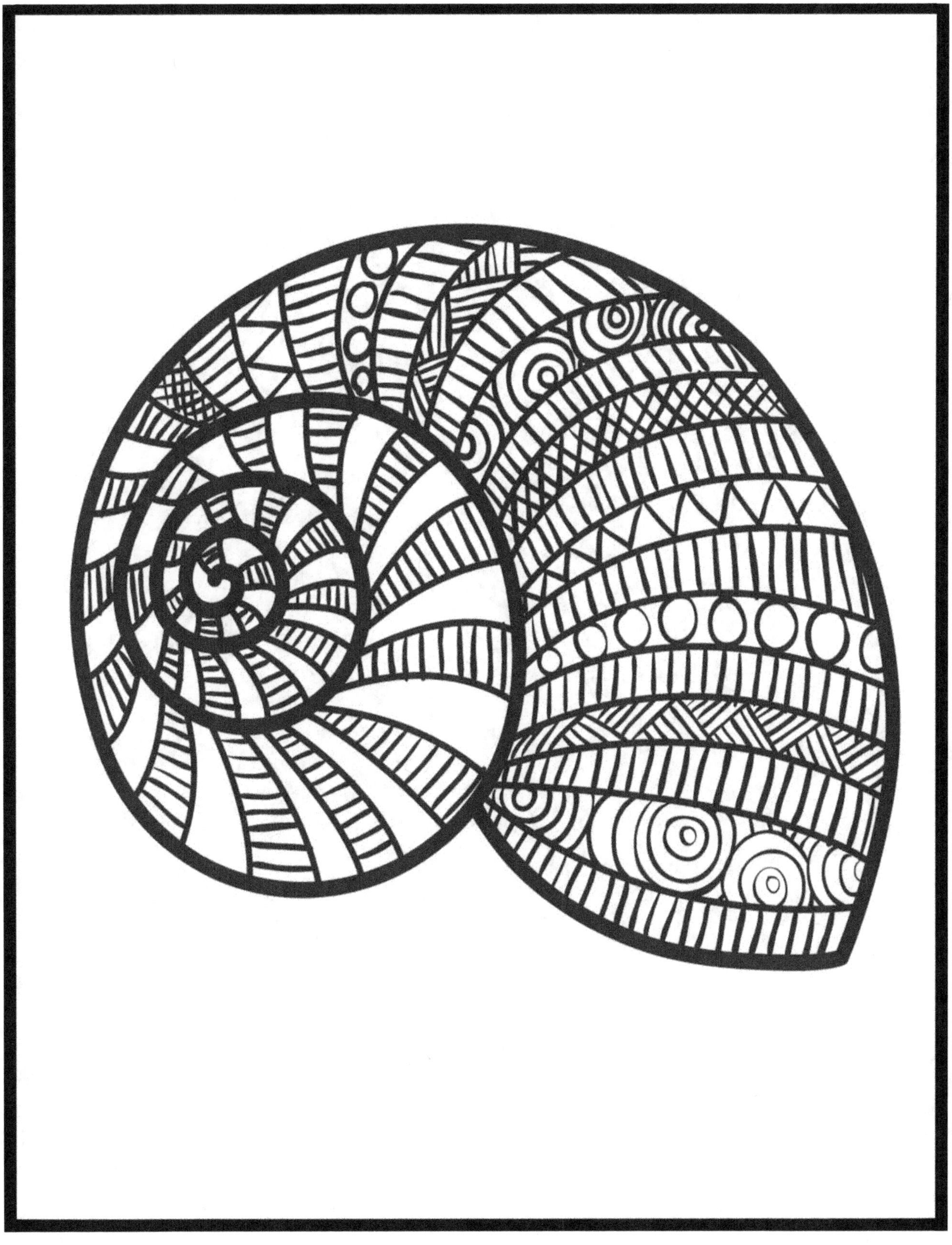

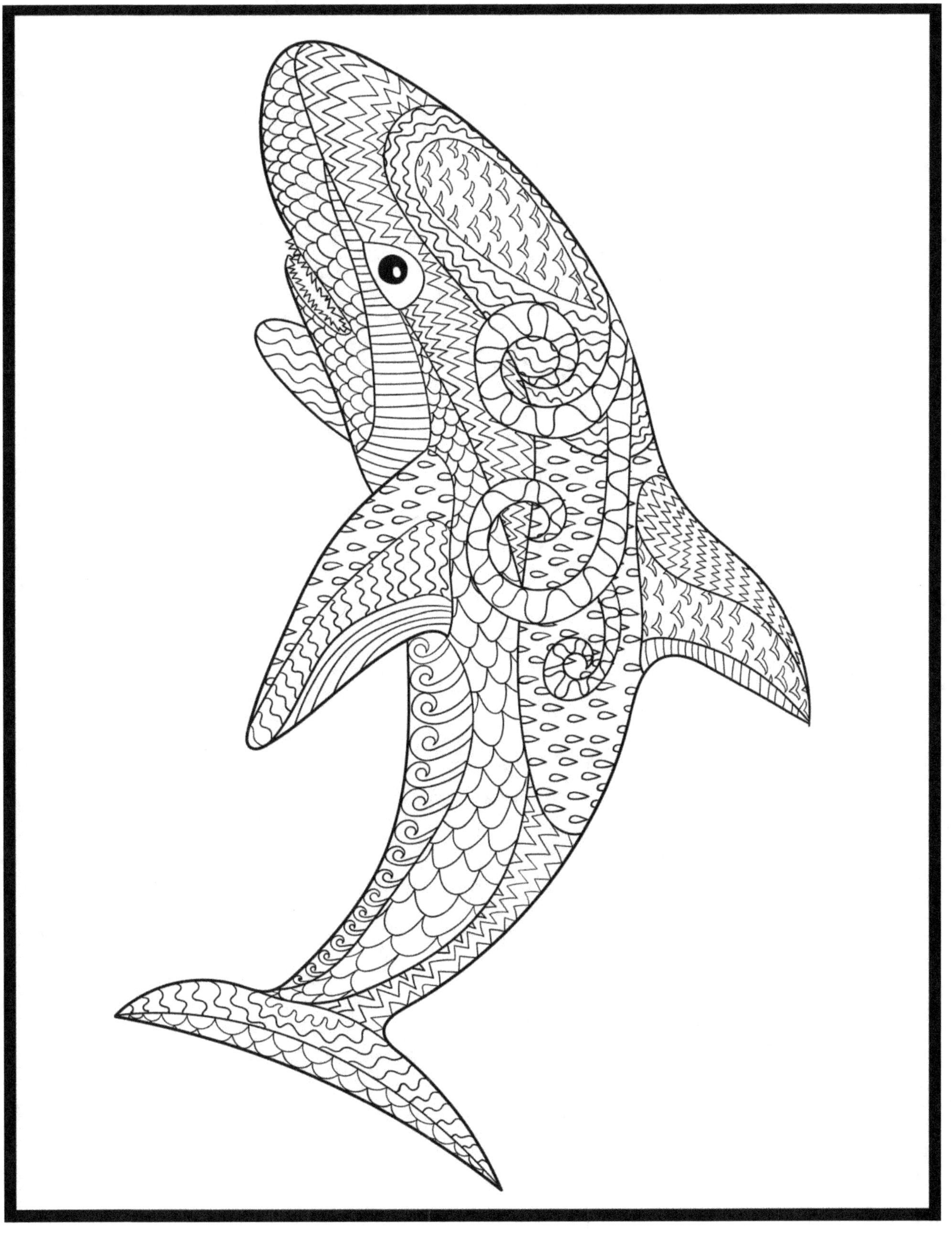

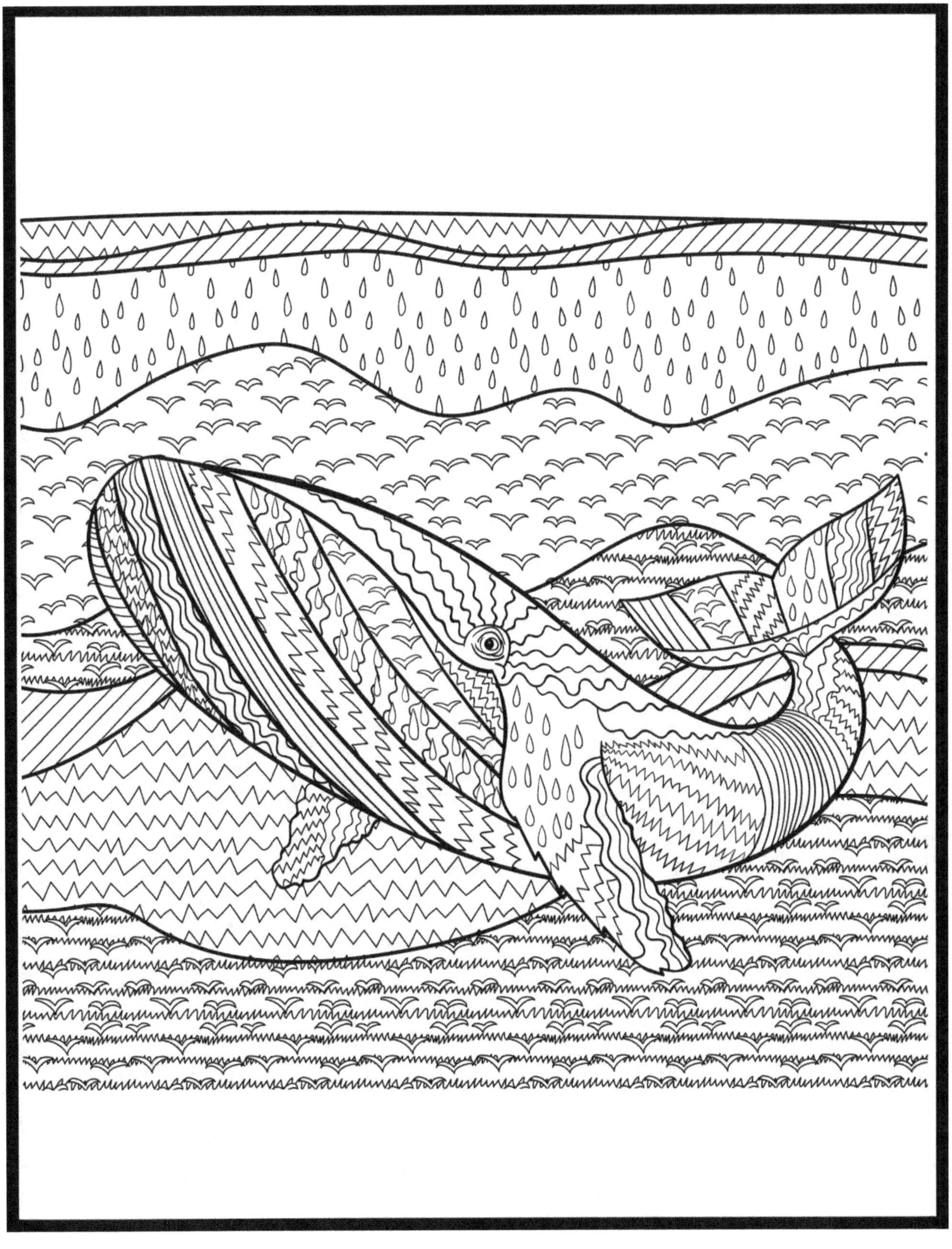

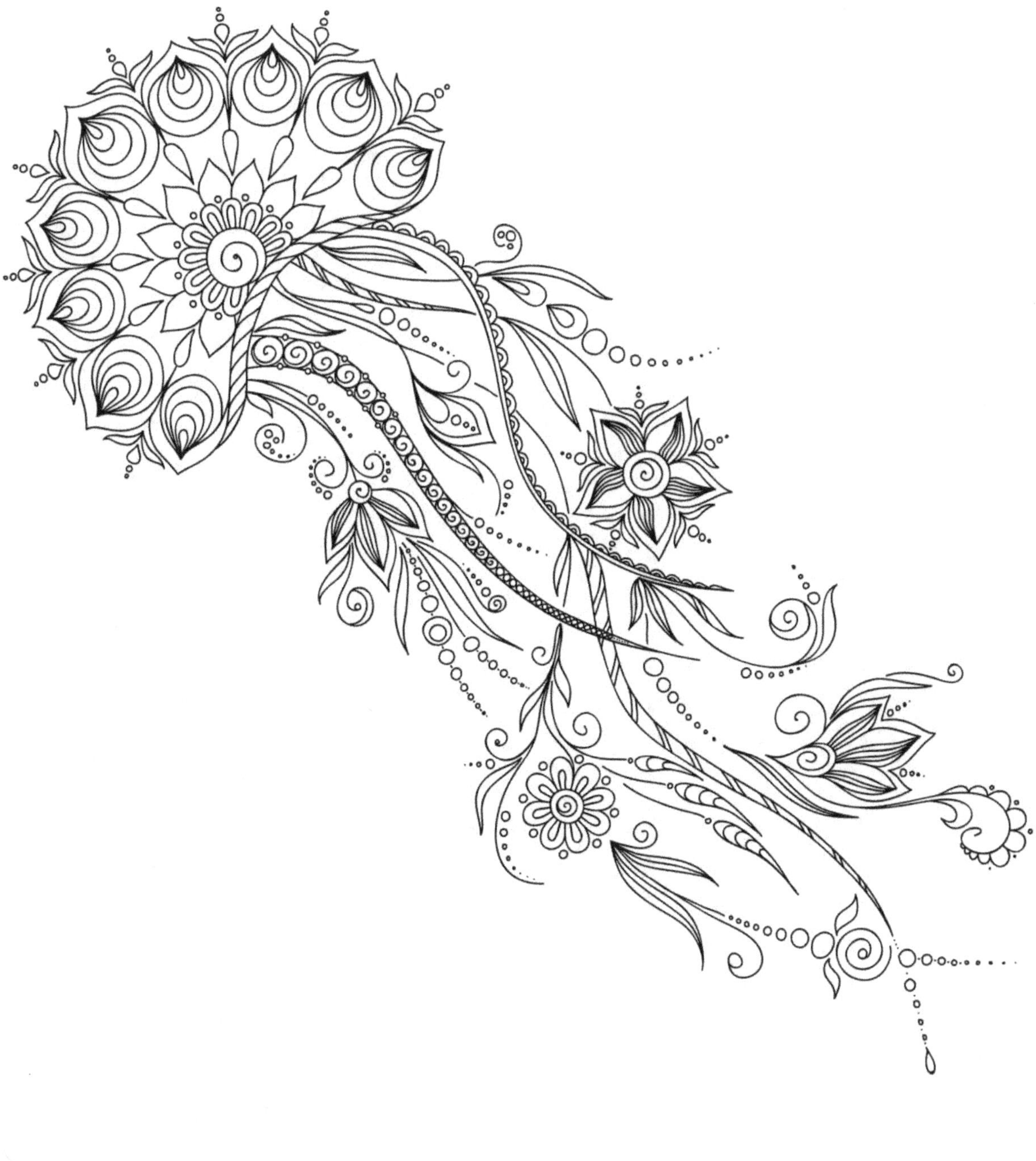

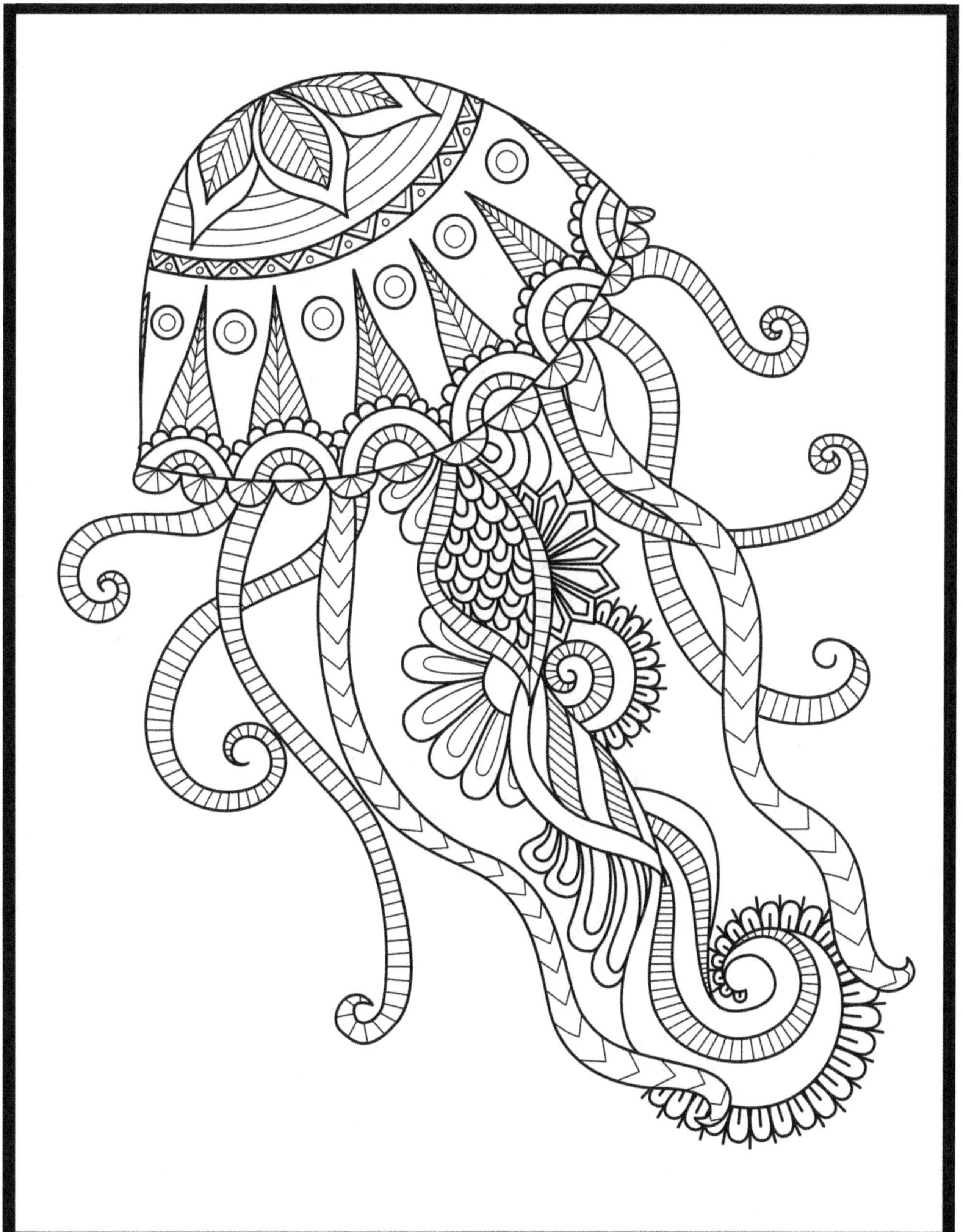

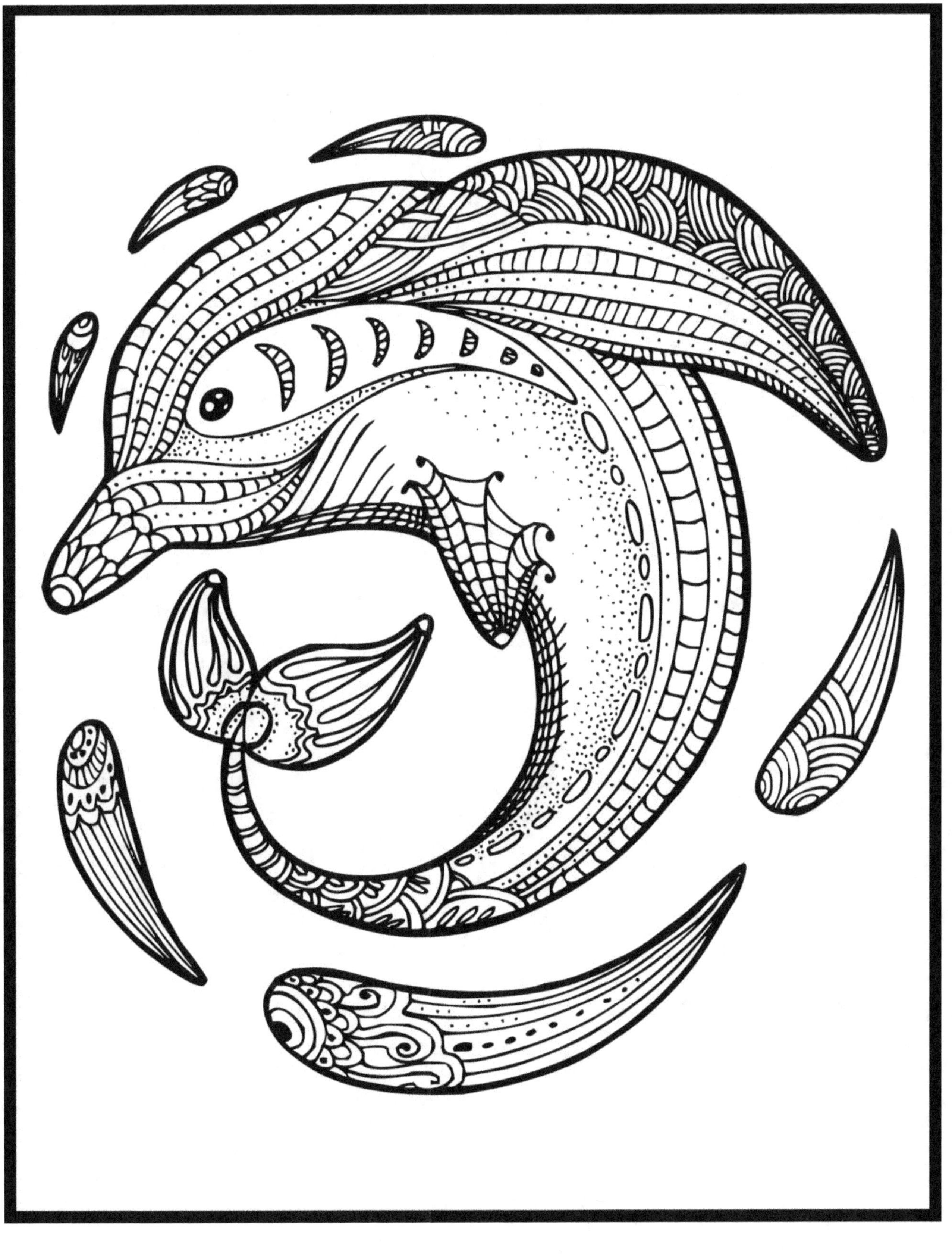

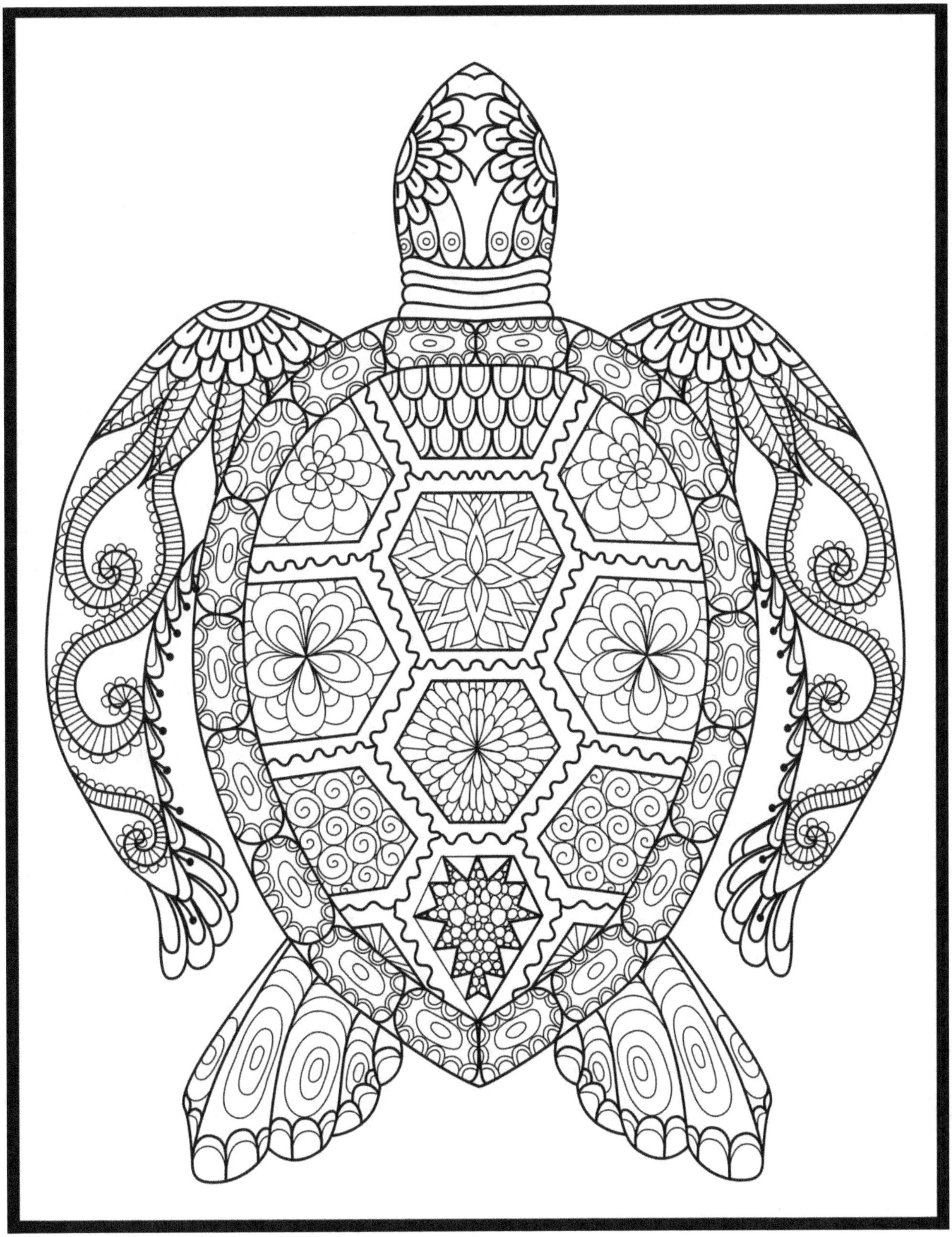

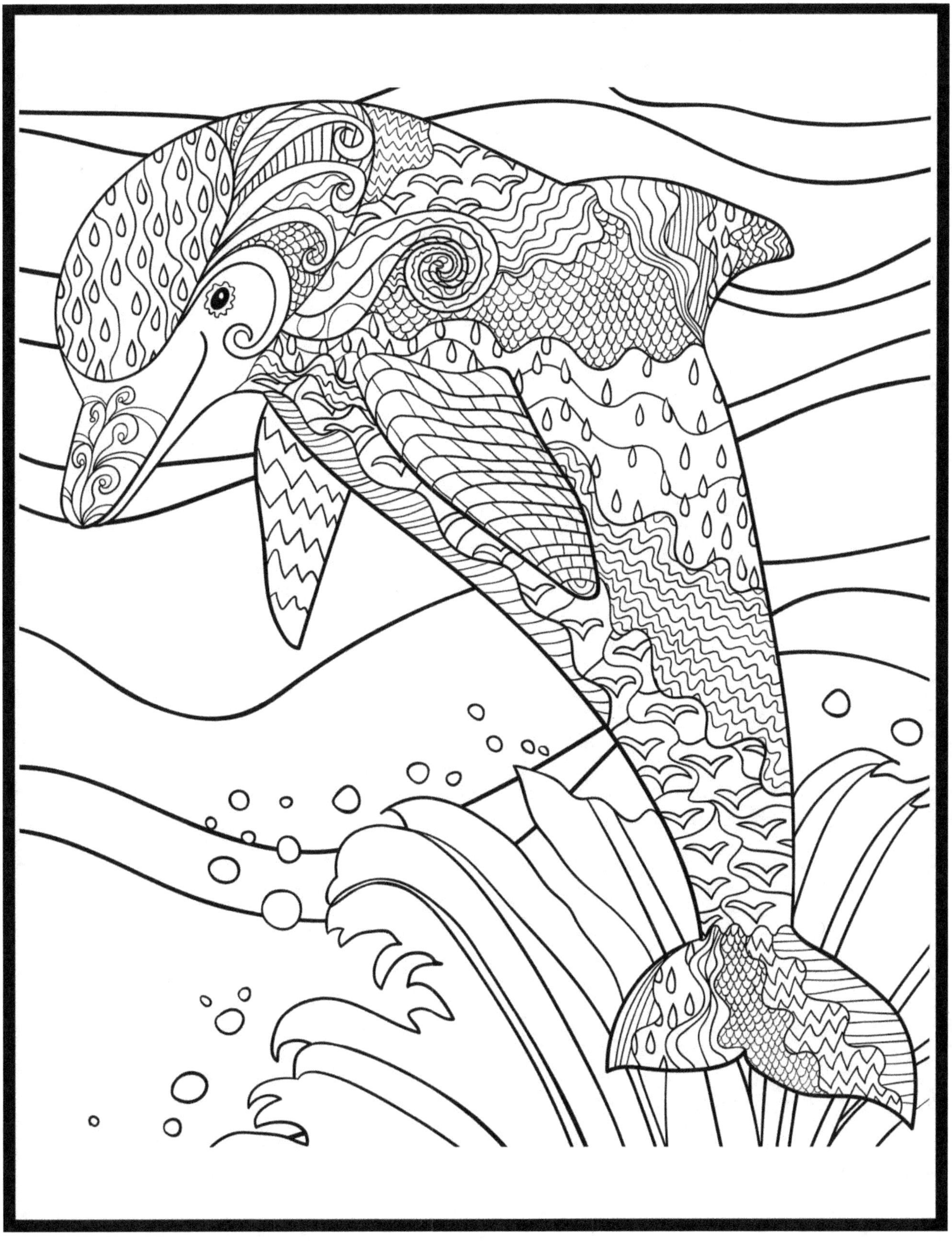

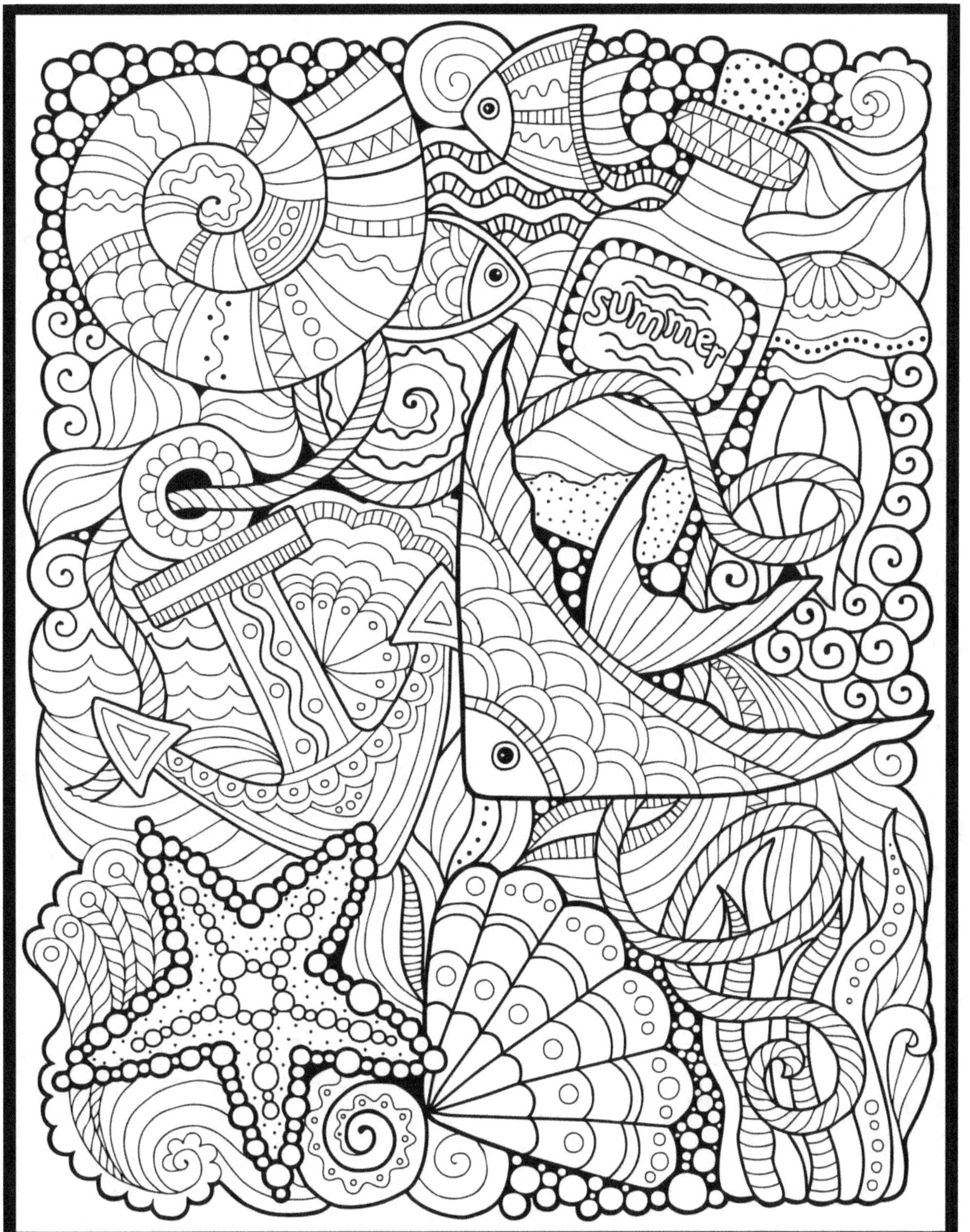
Summer

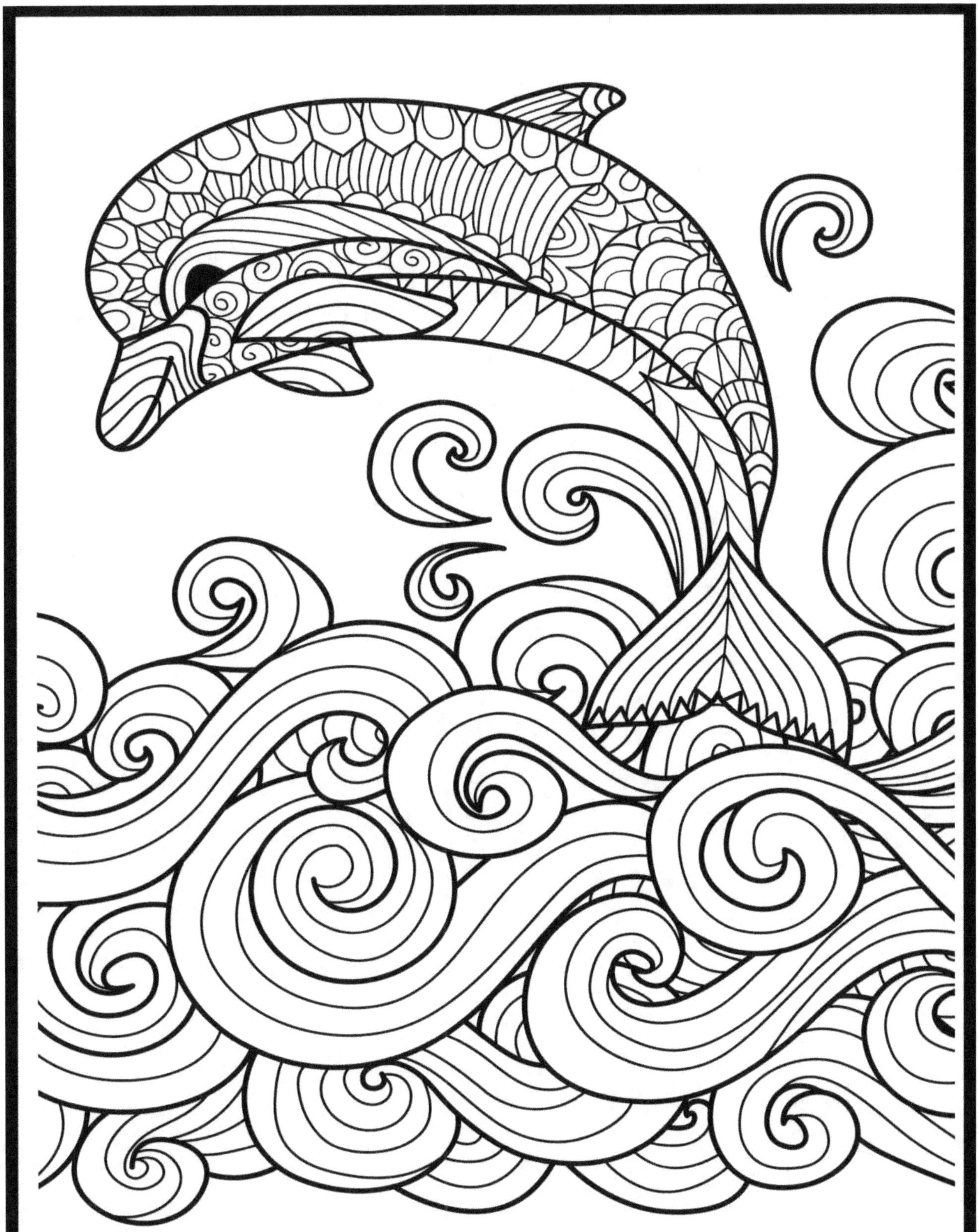

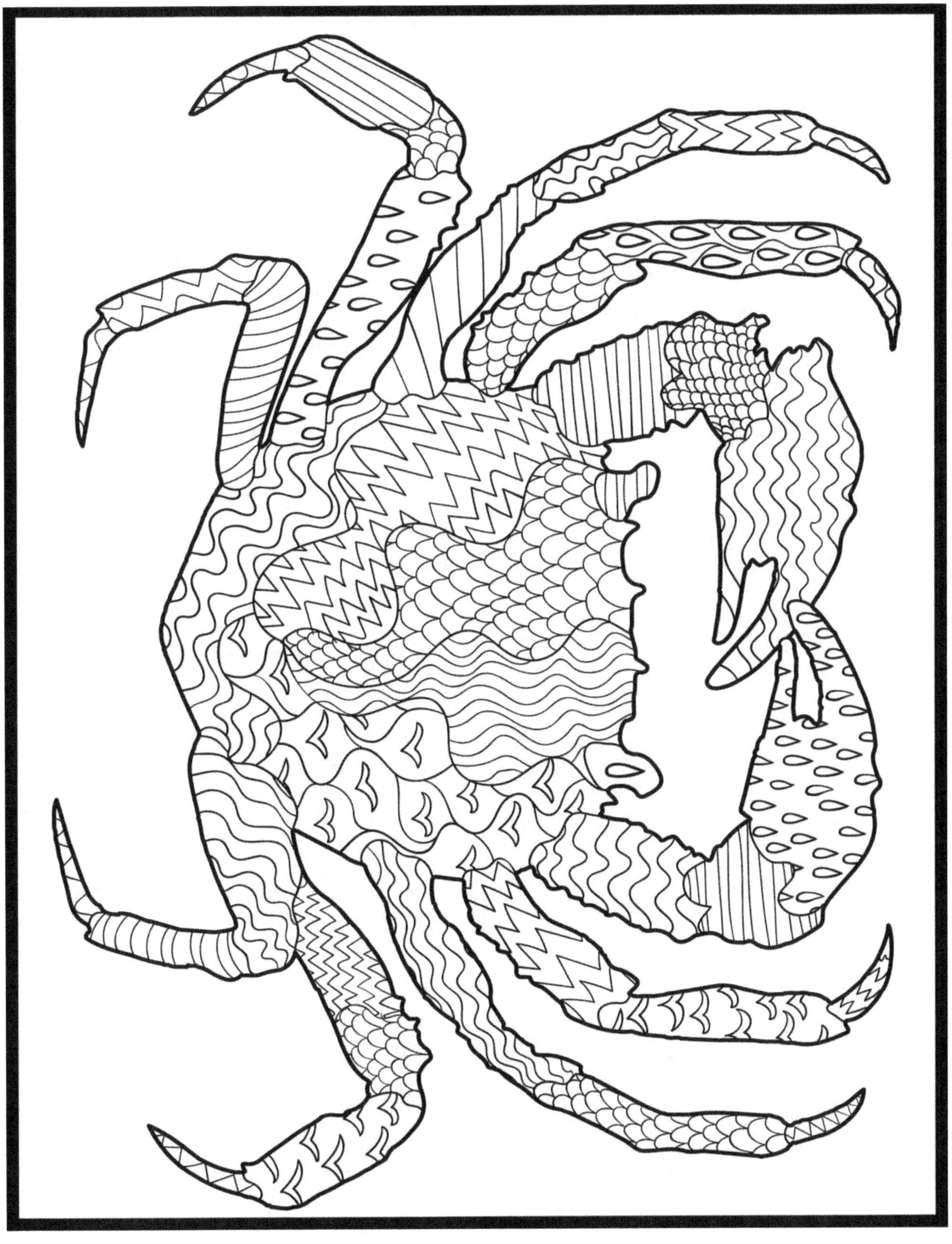

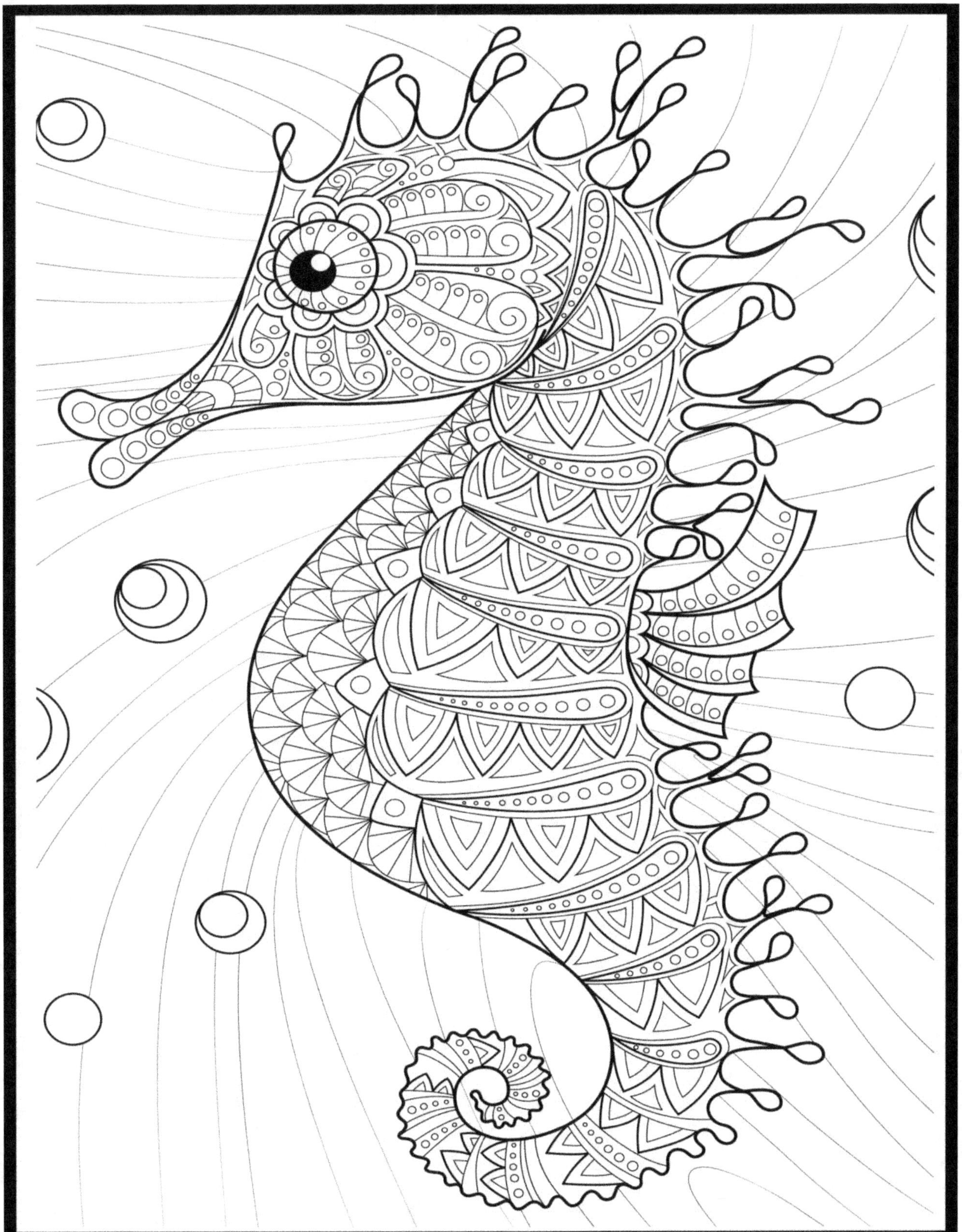

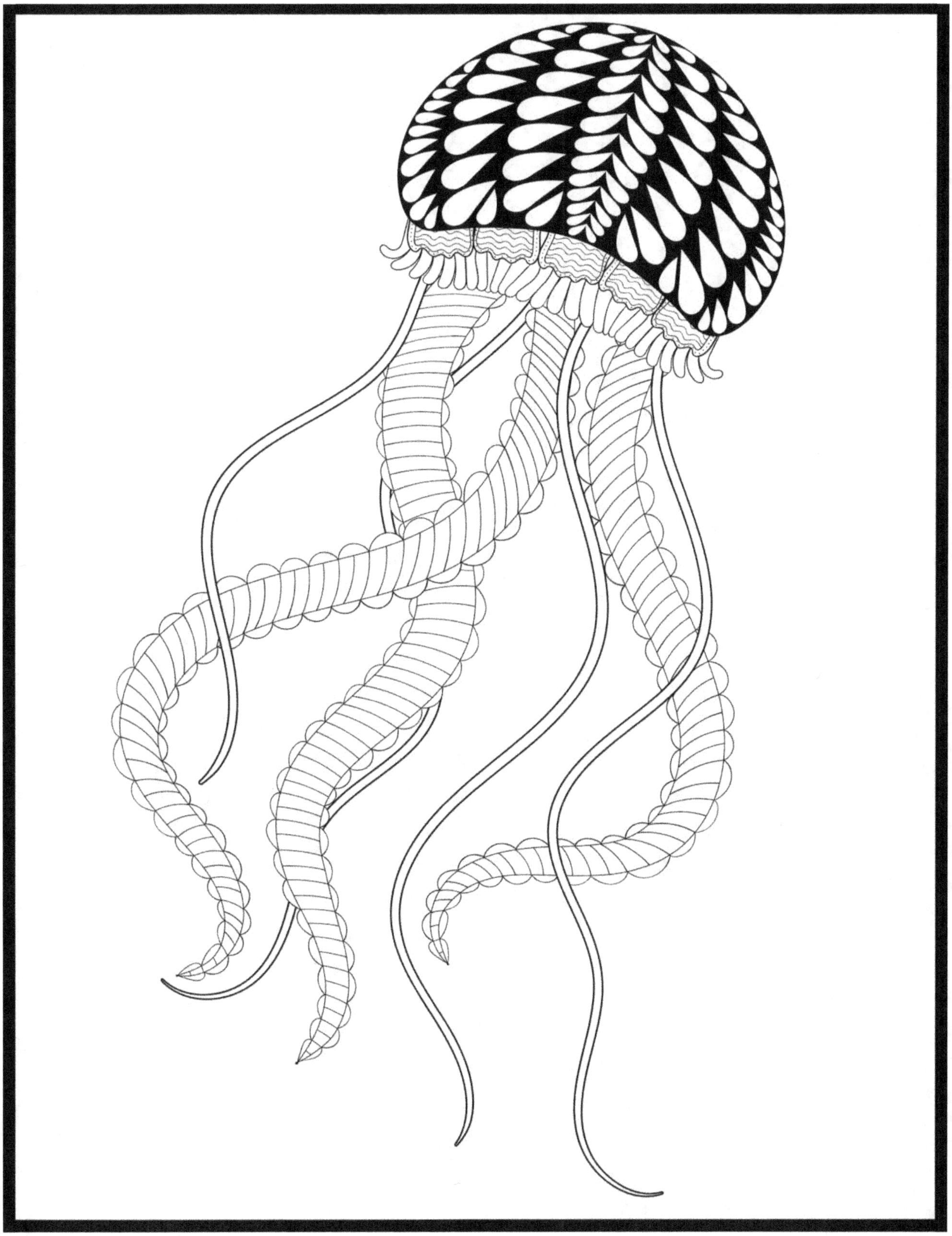

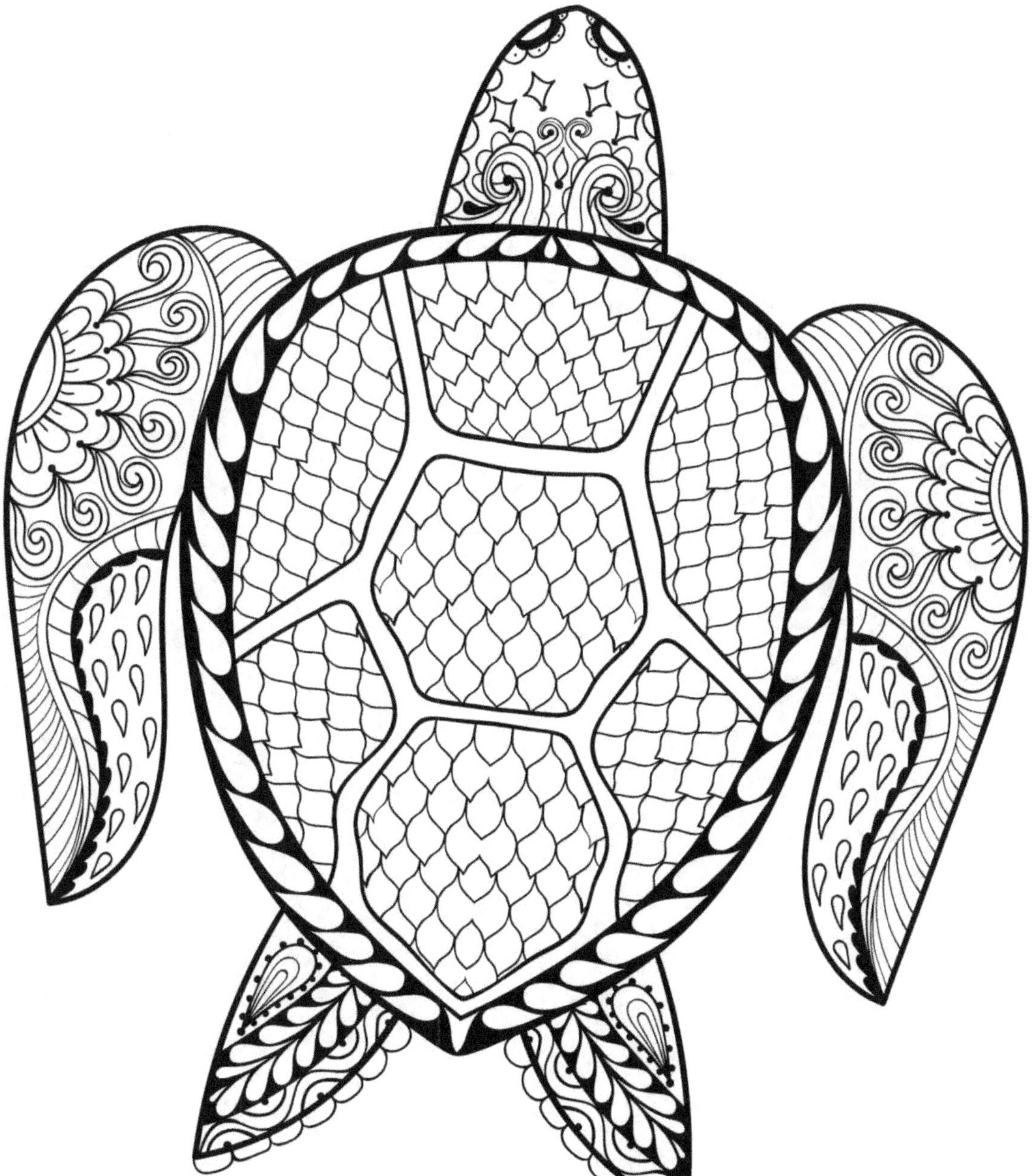

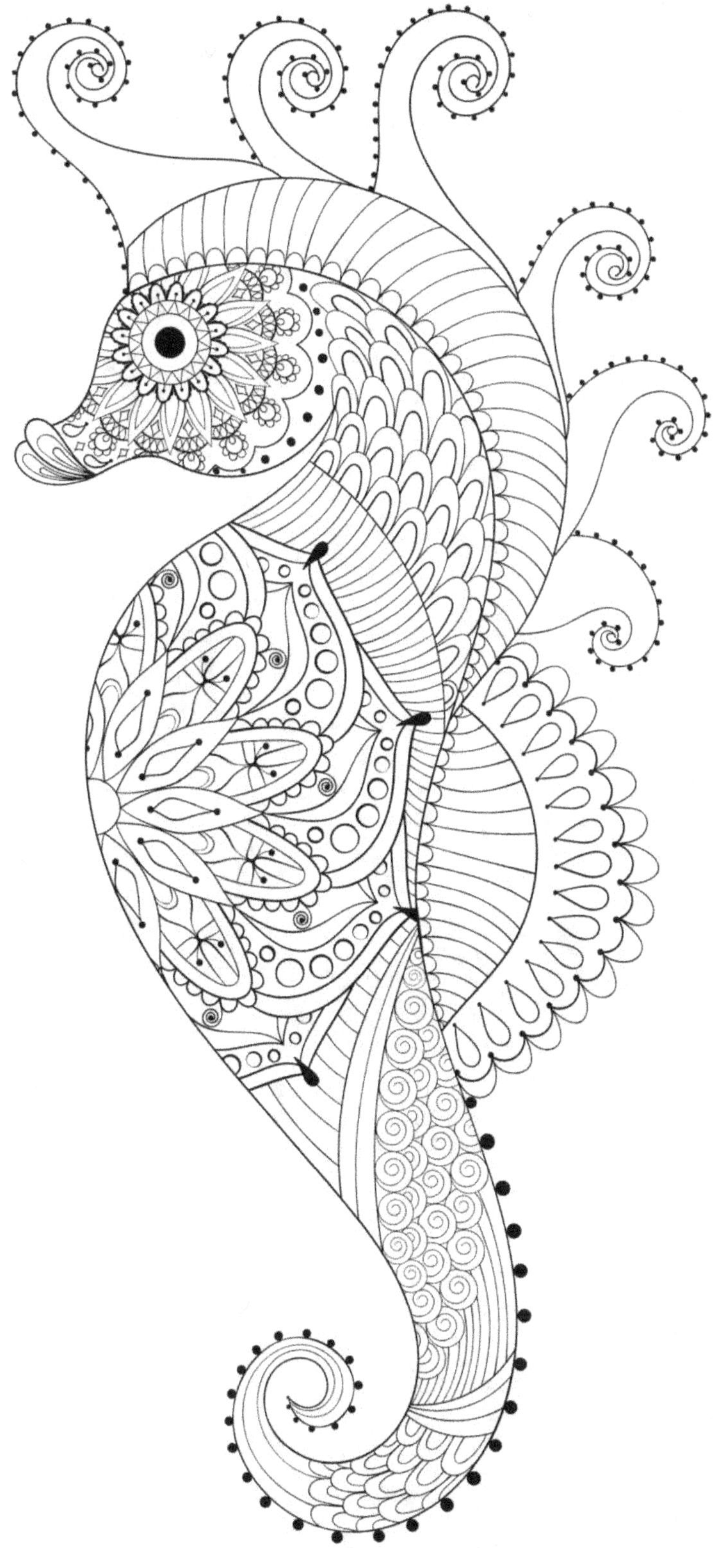

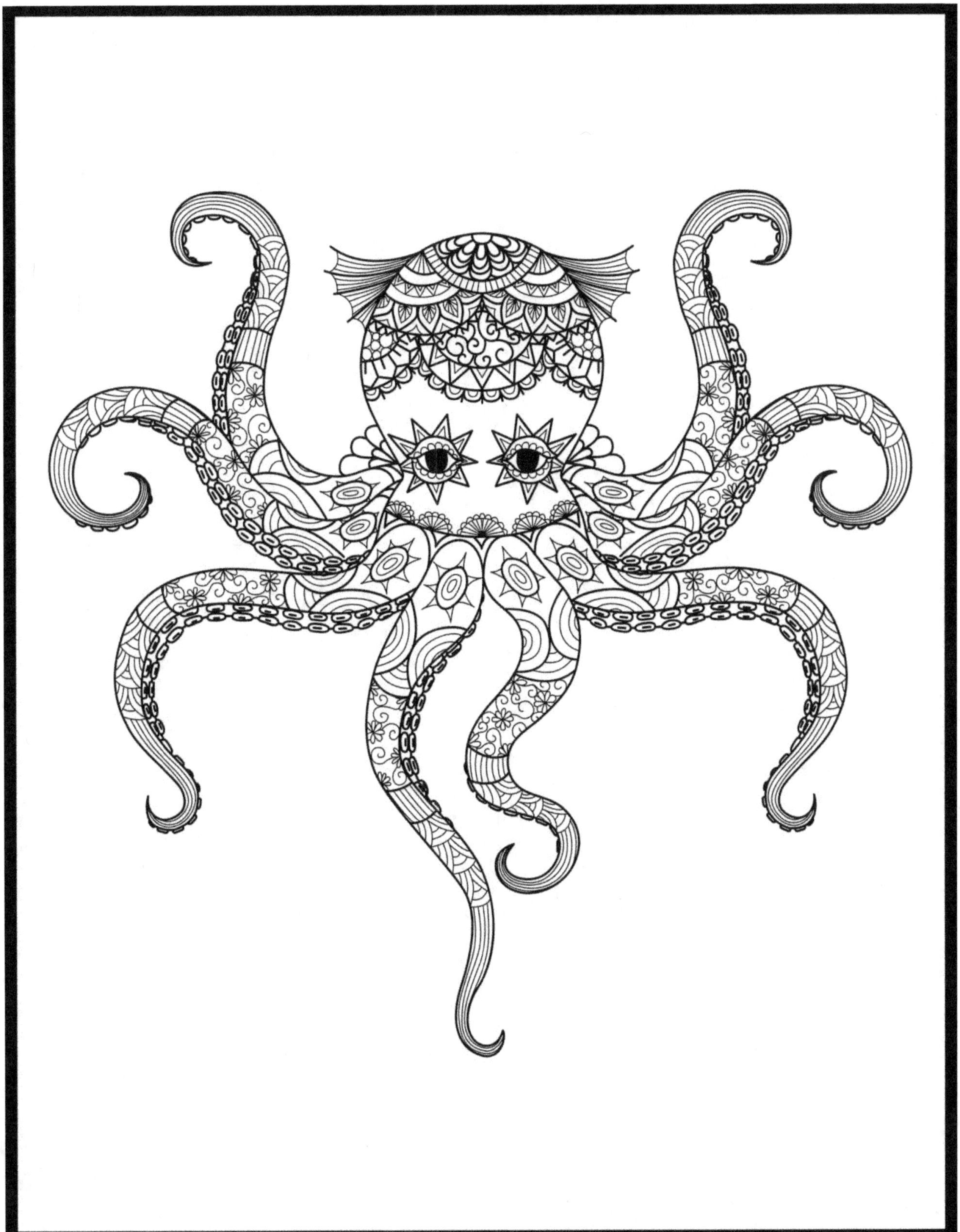

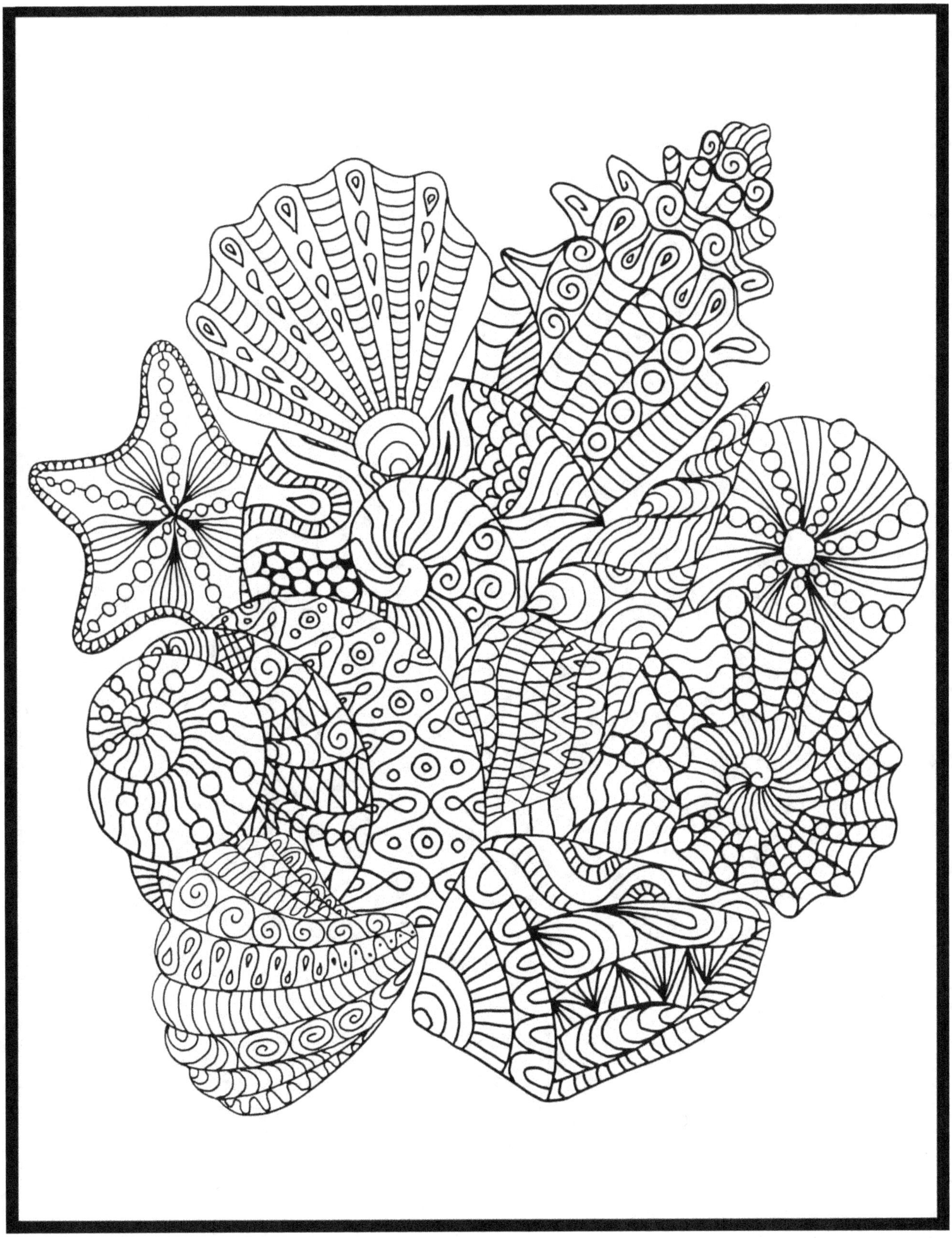

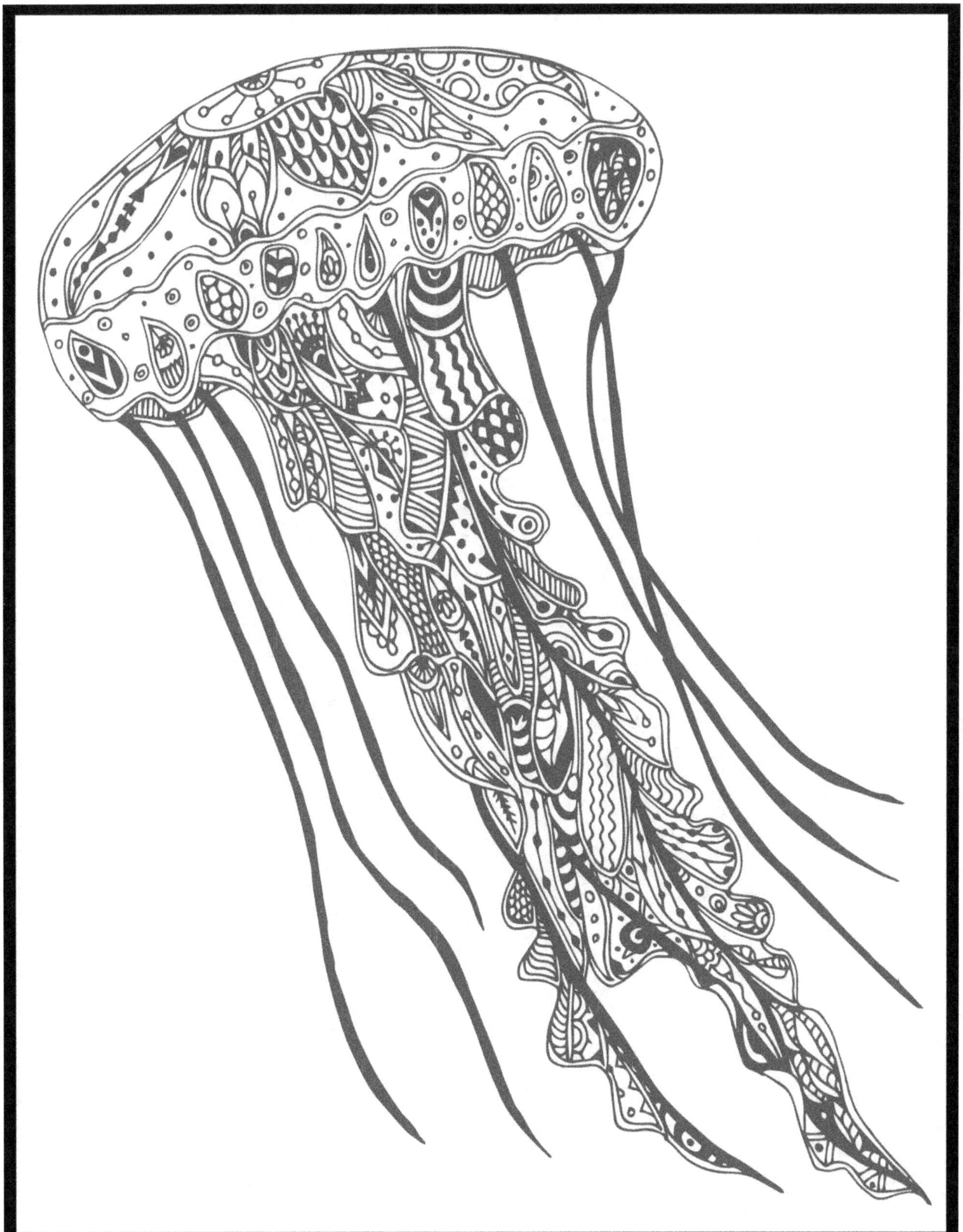

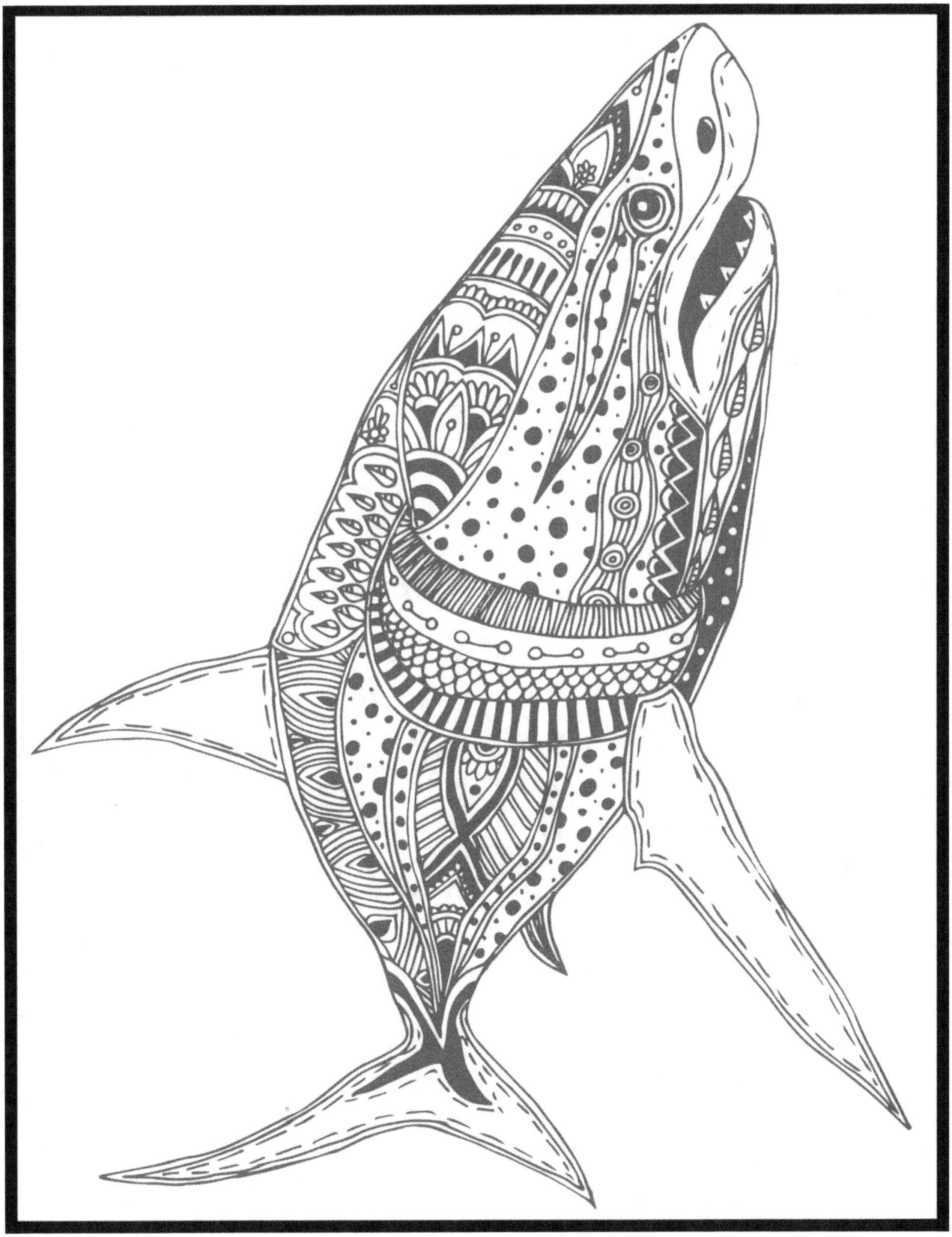

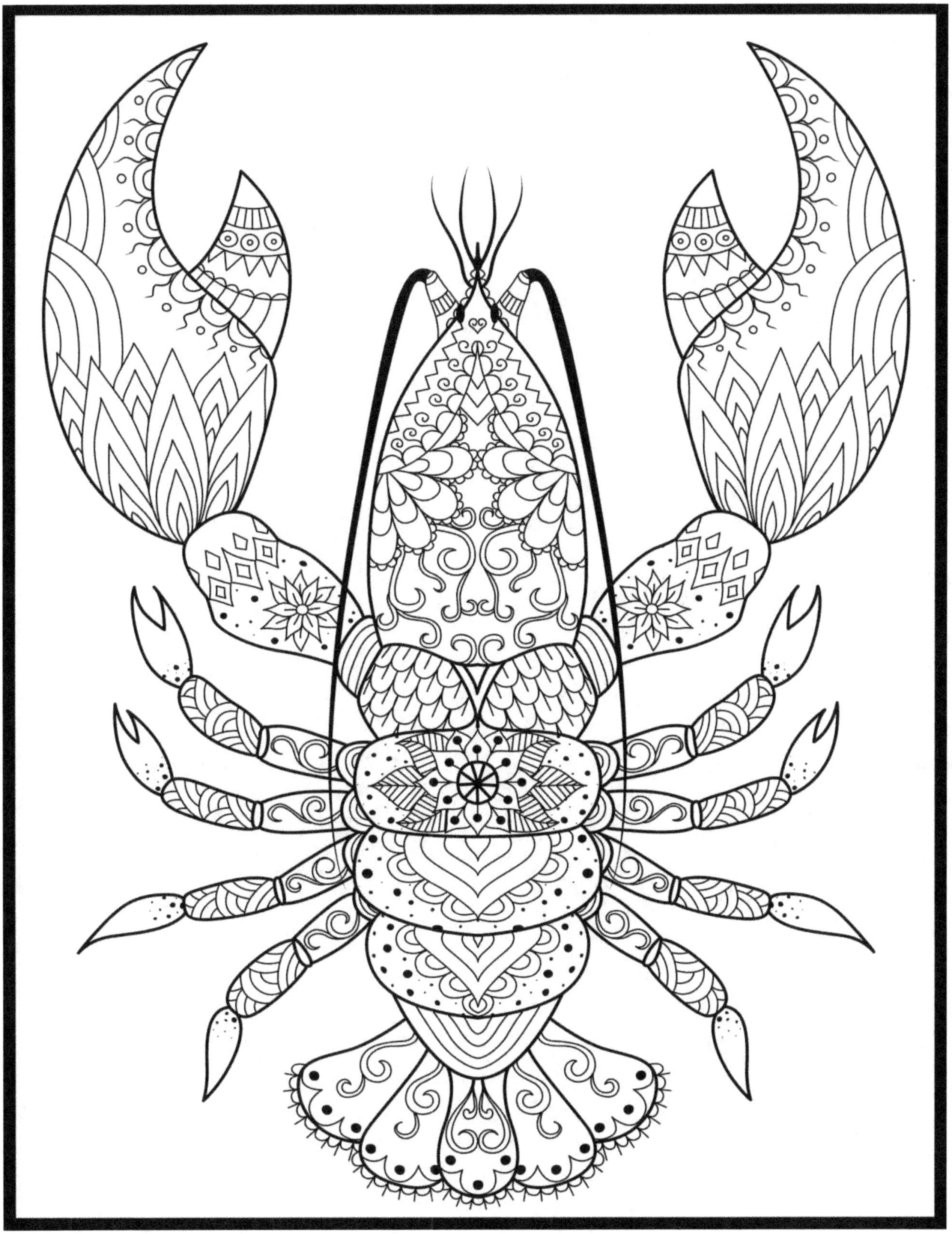

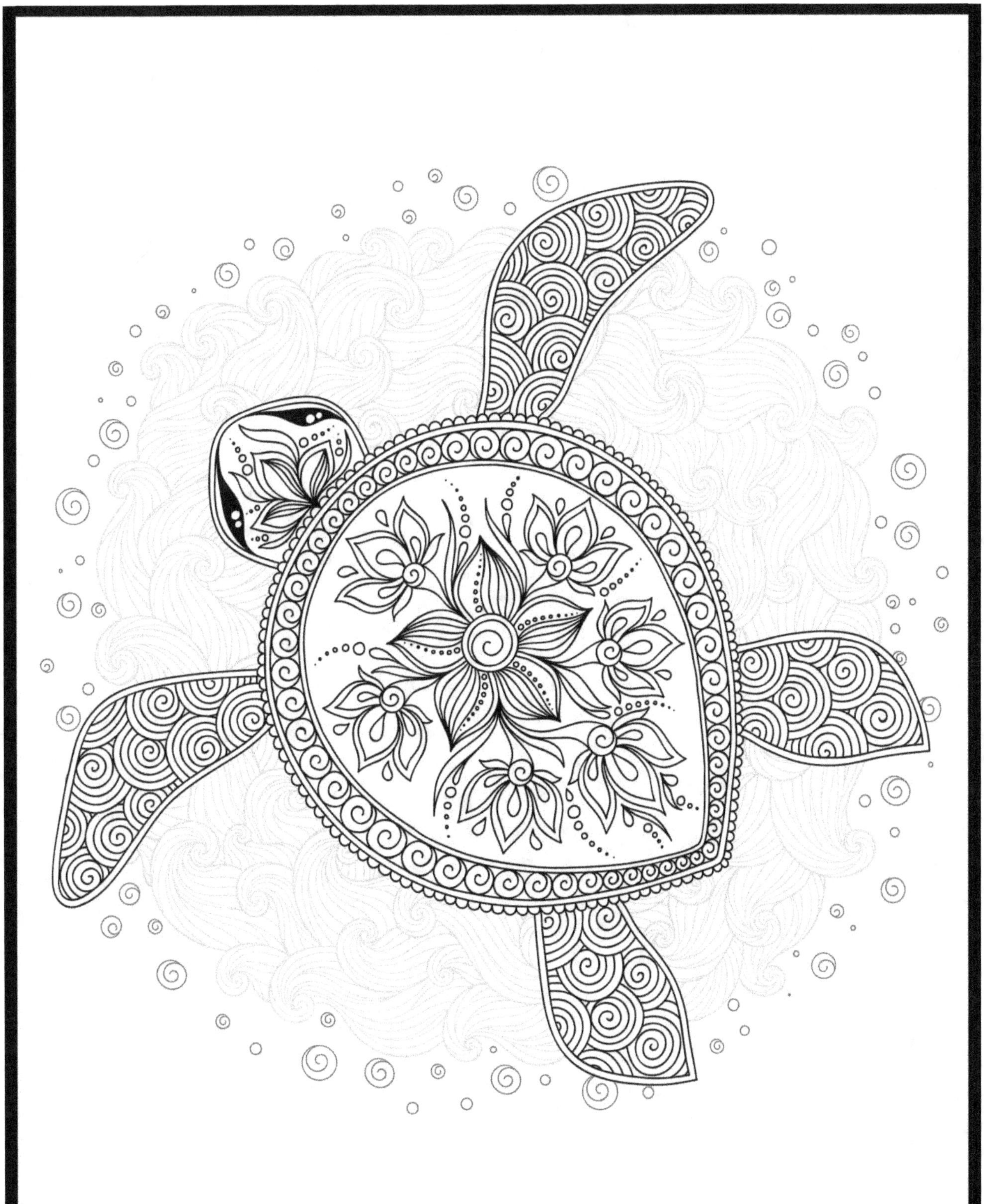

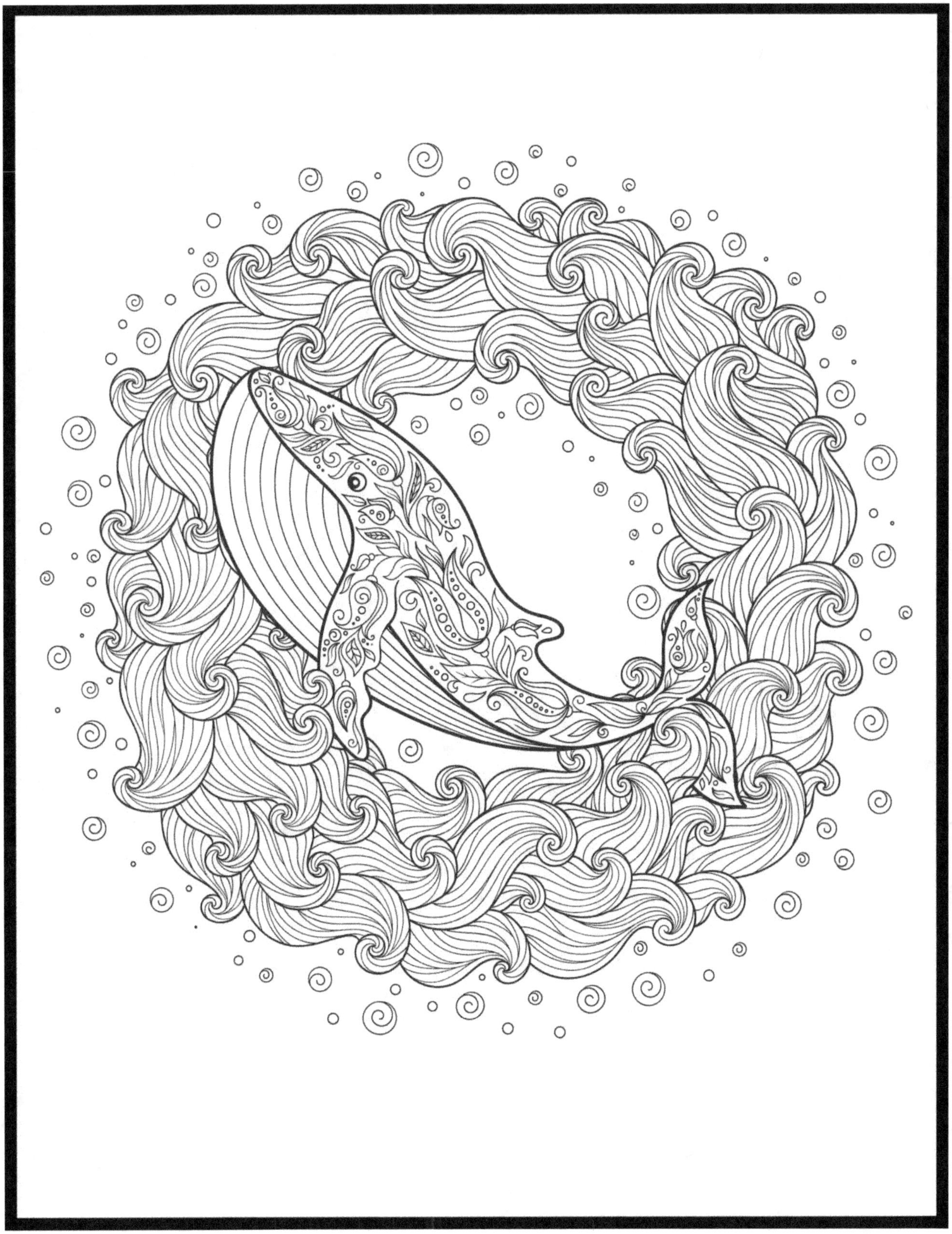

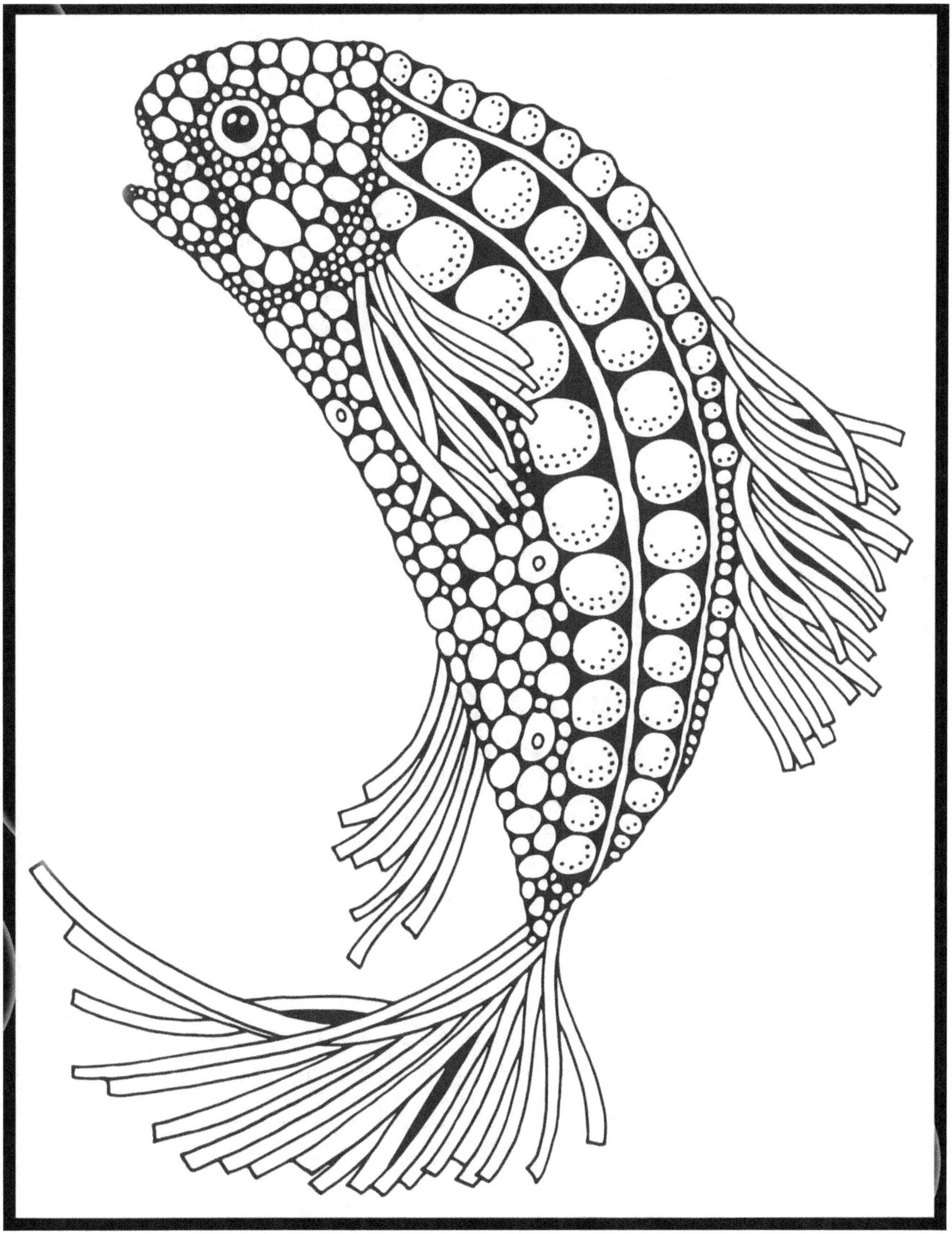

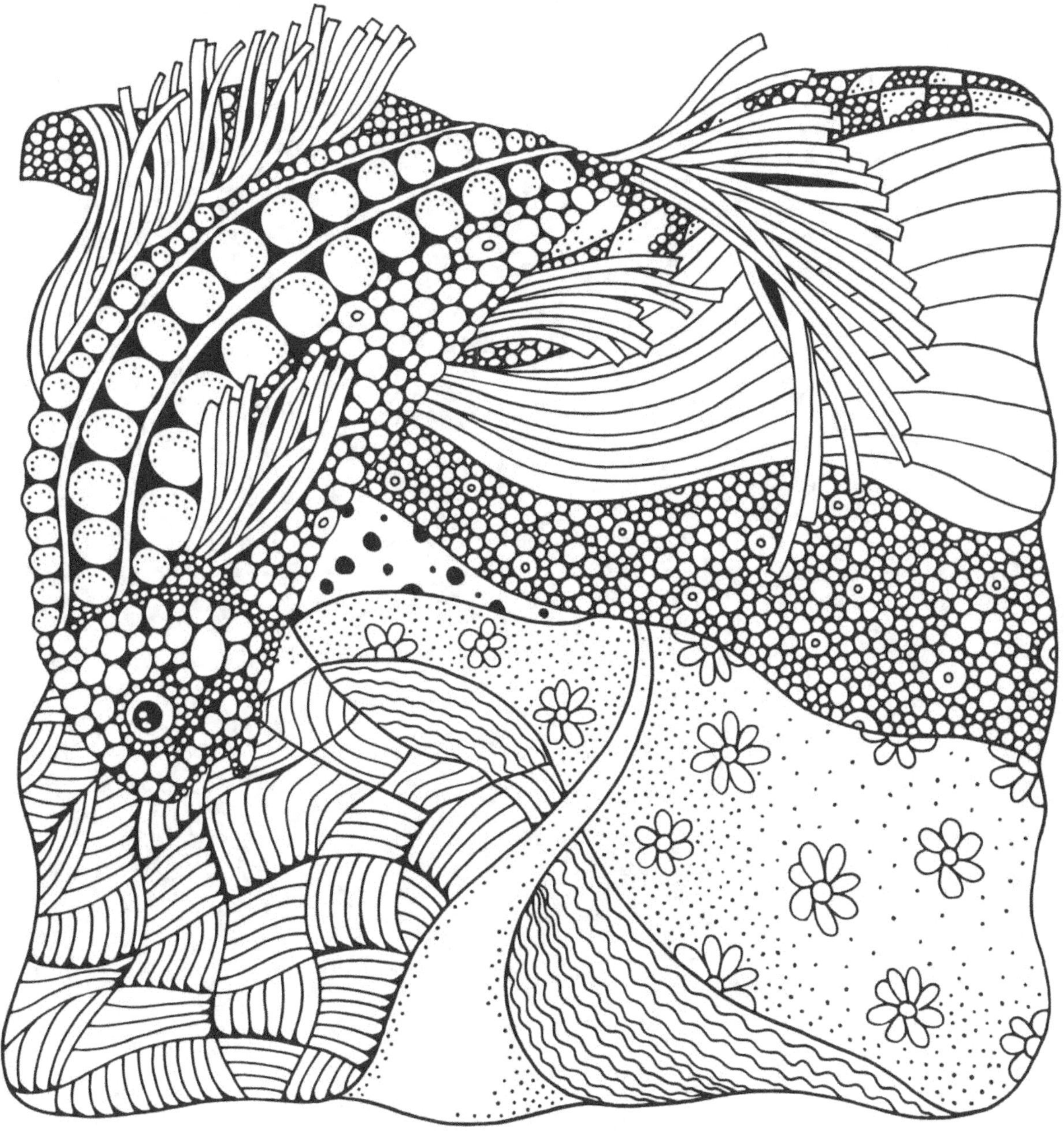

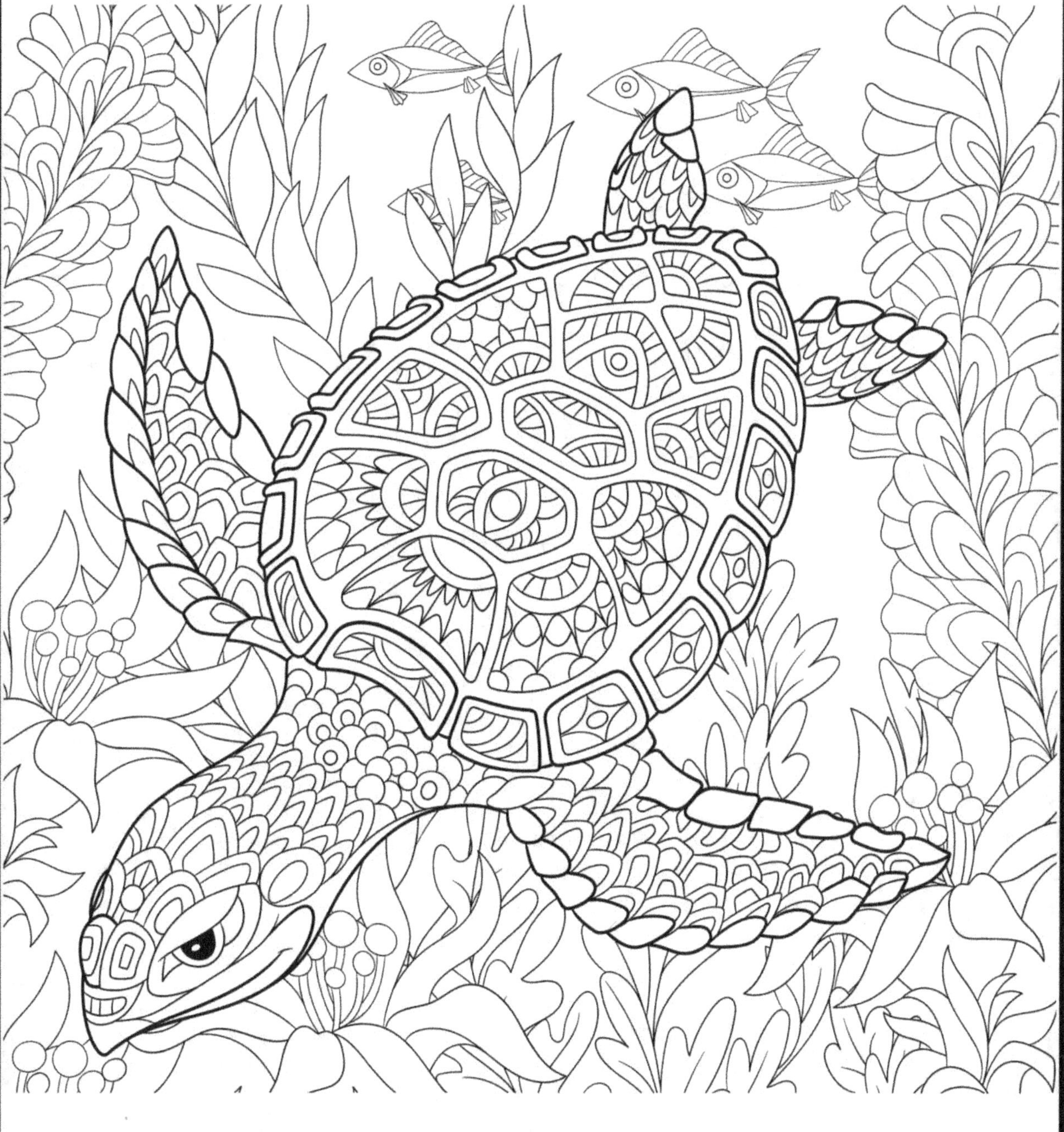

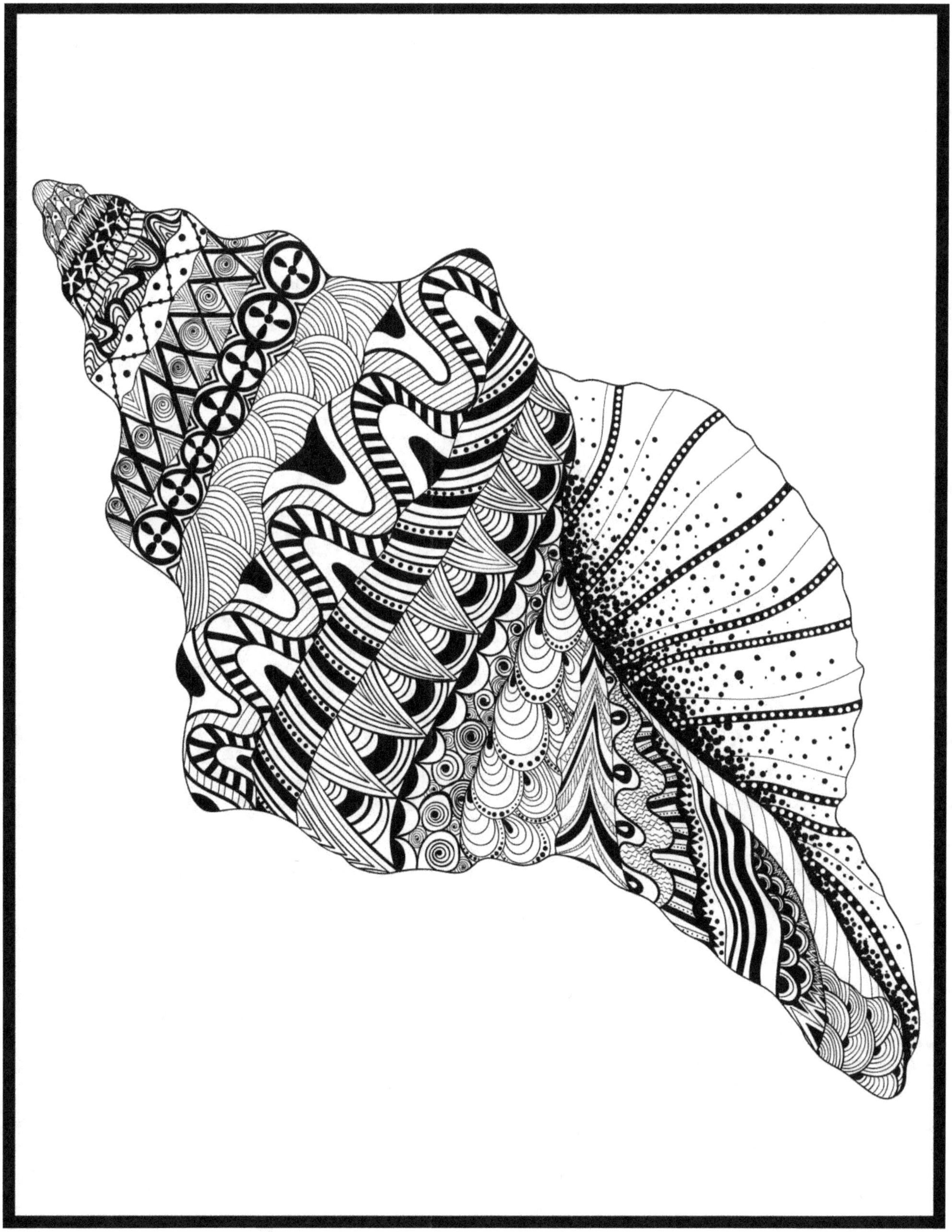

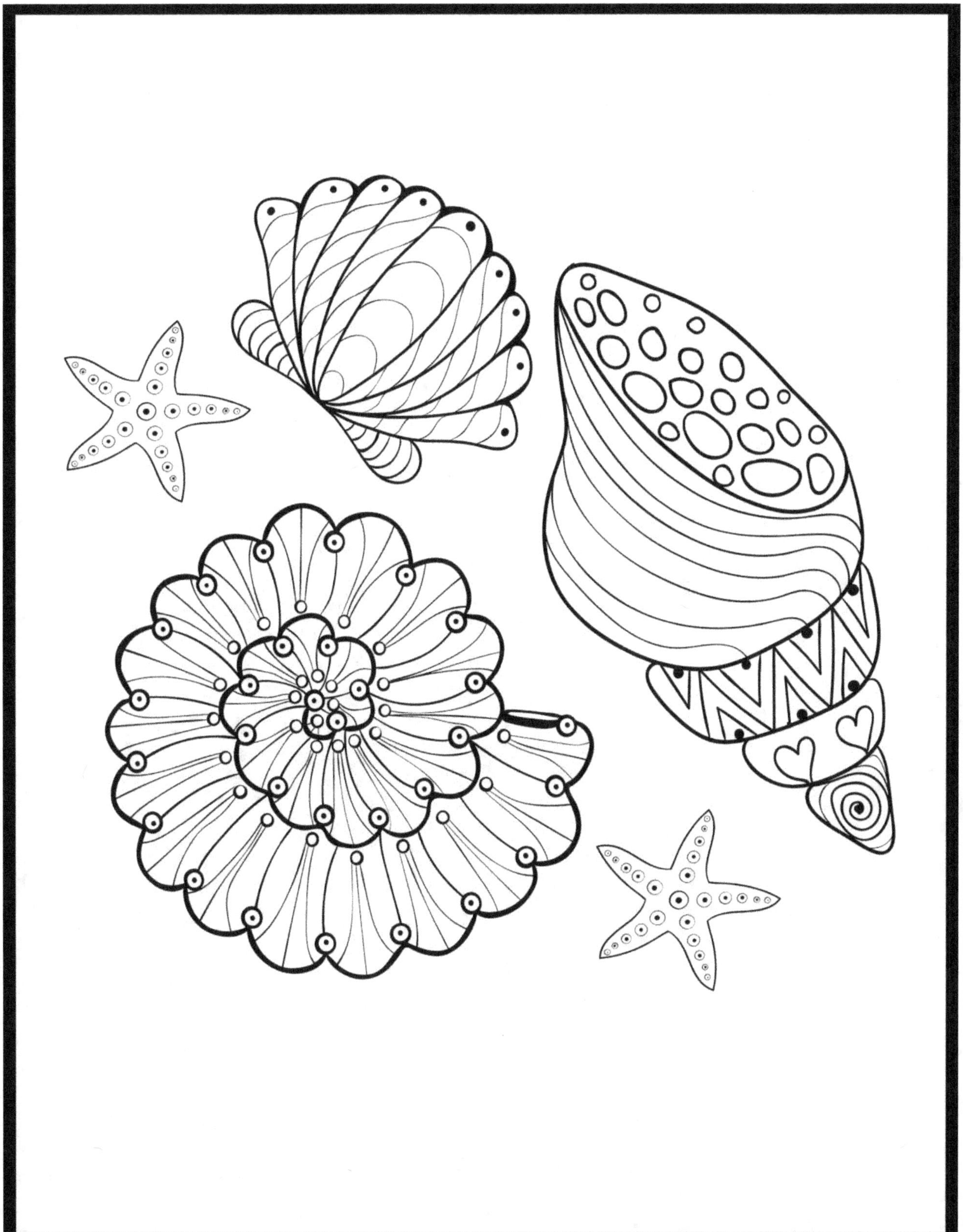

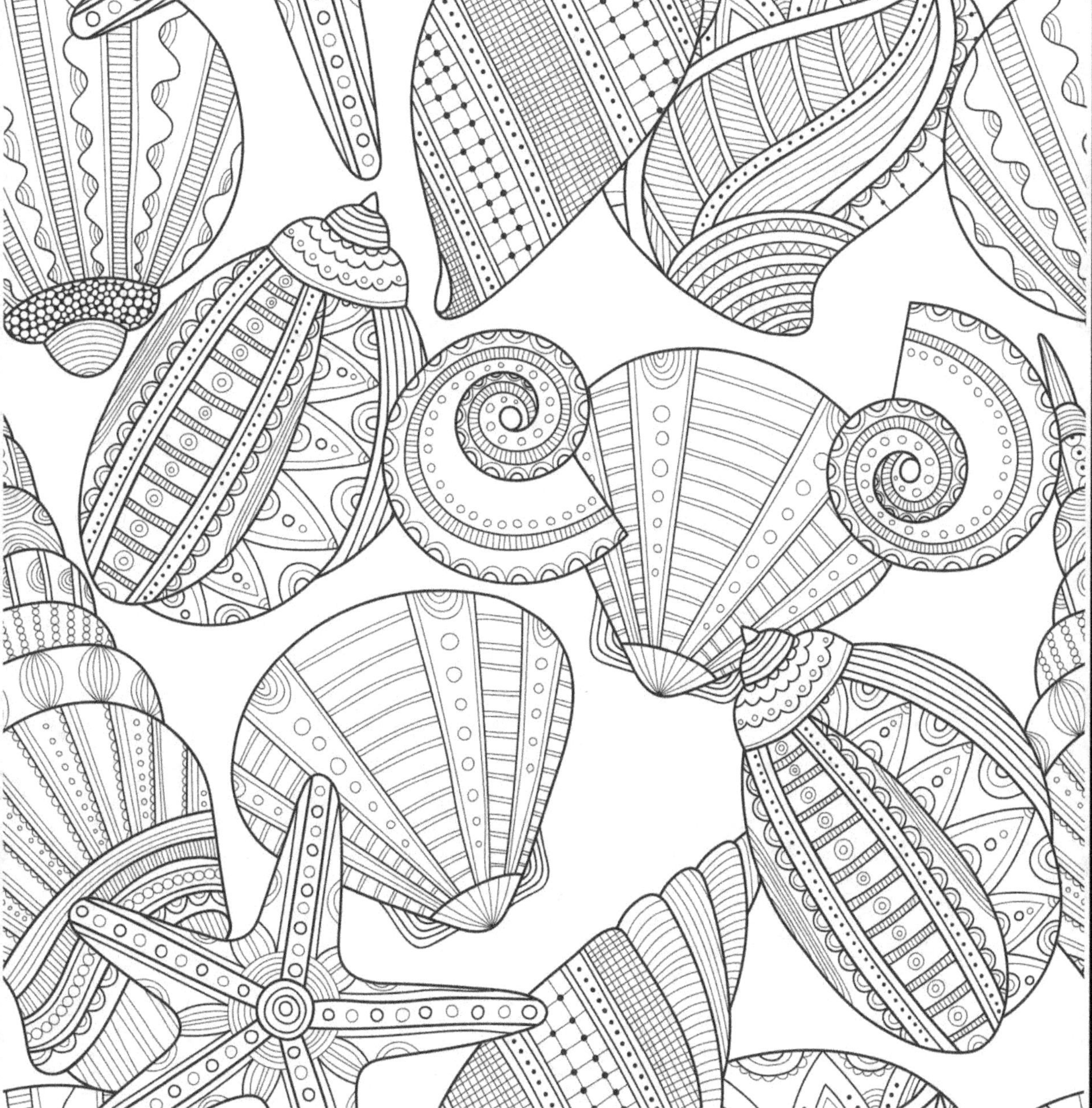

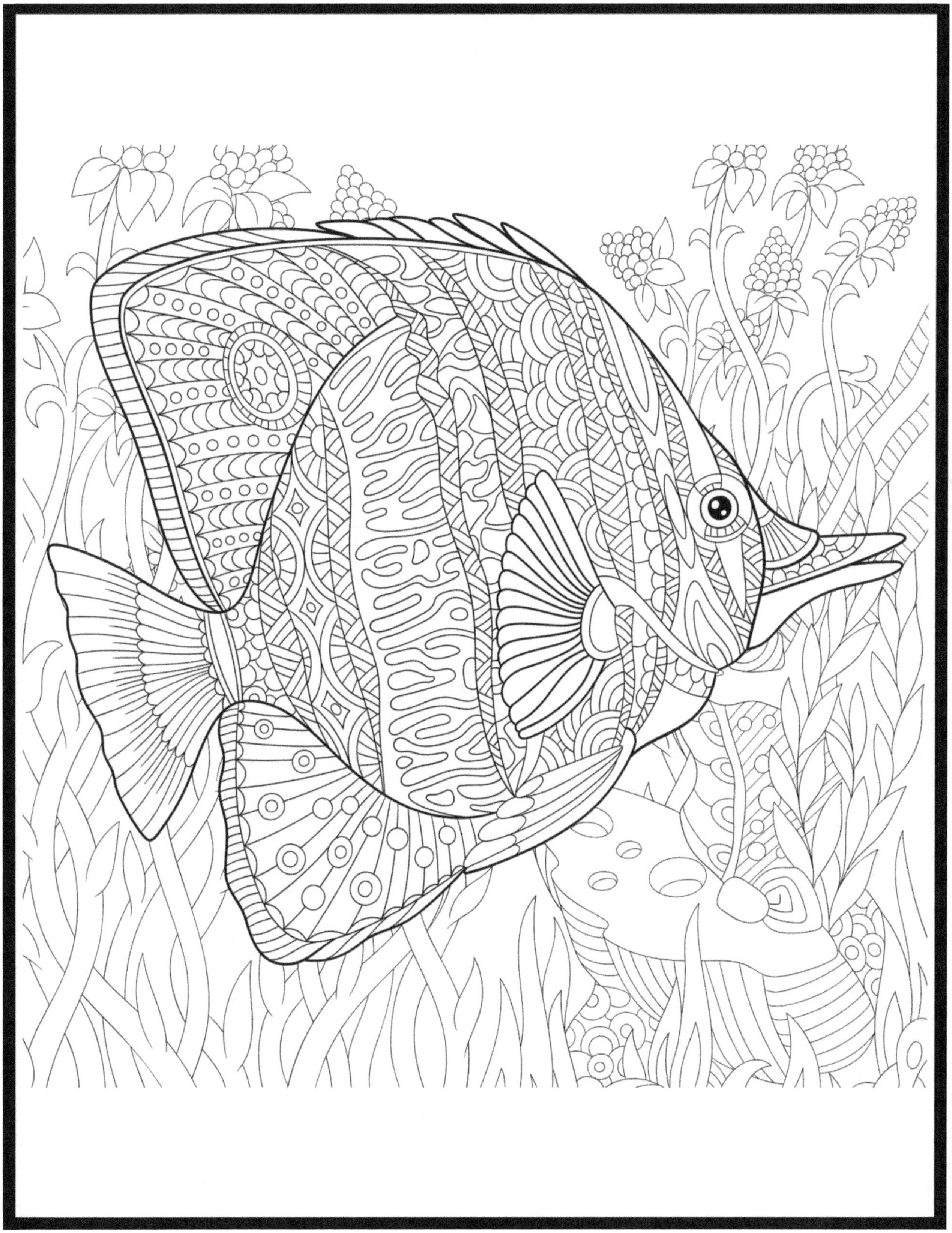

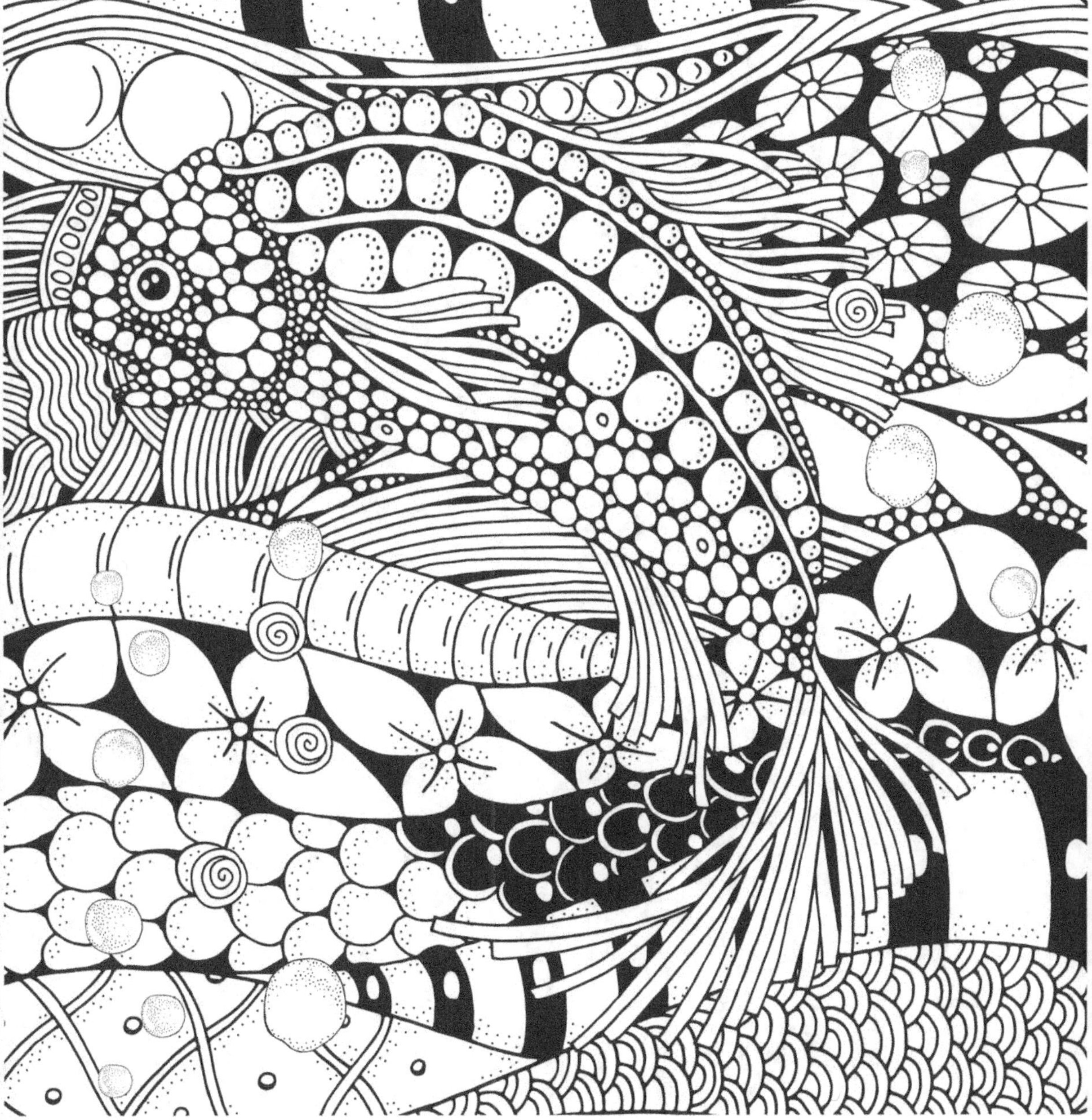

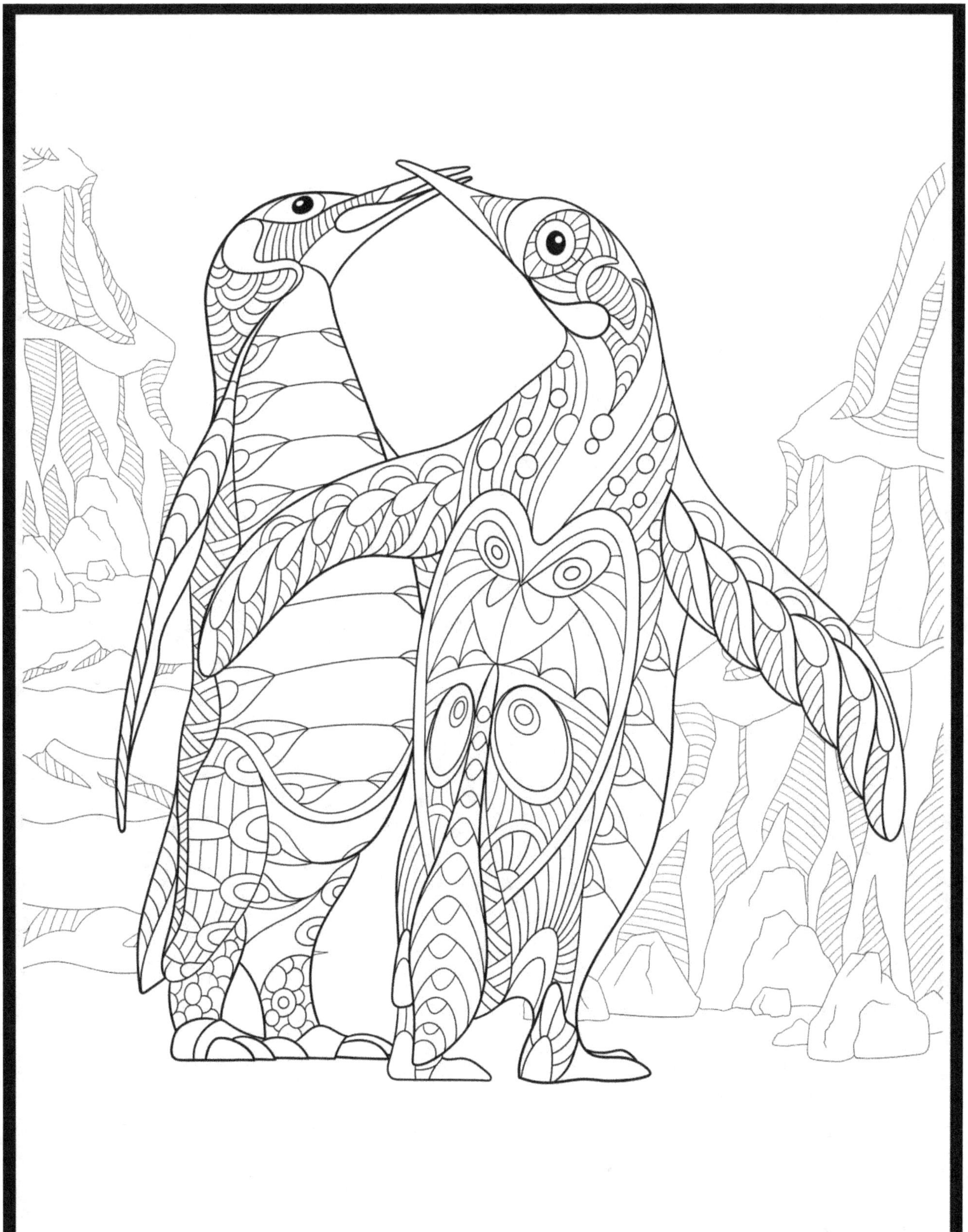

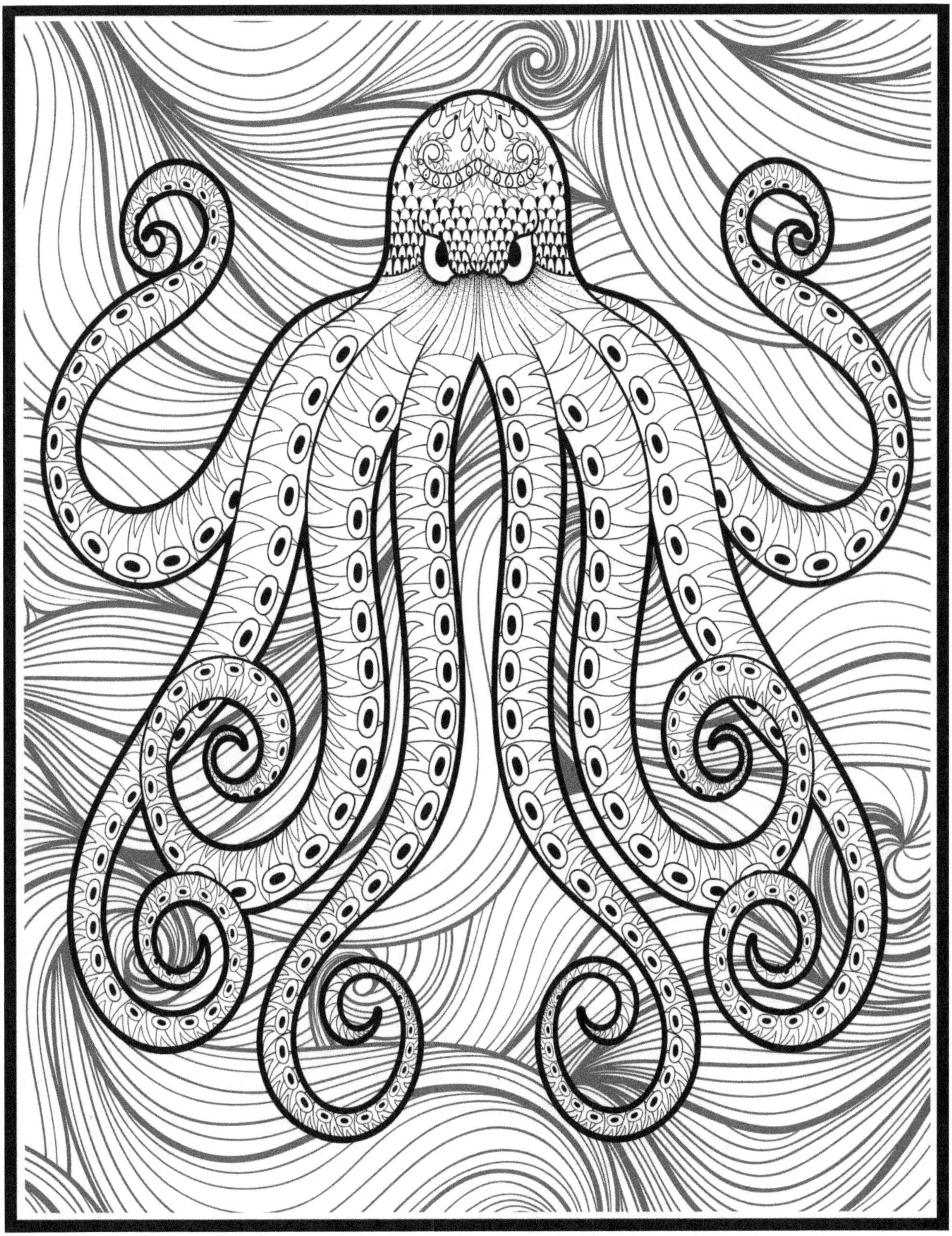

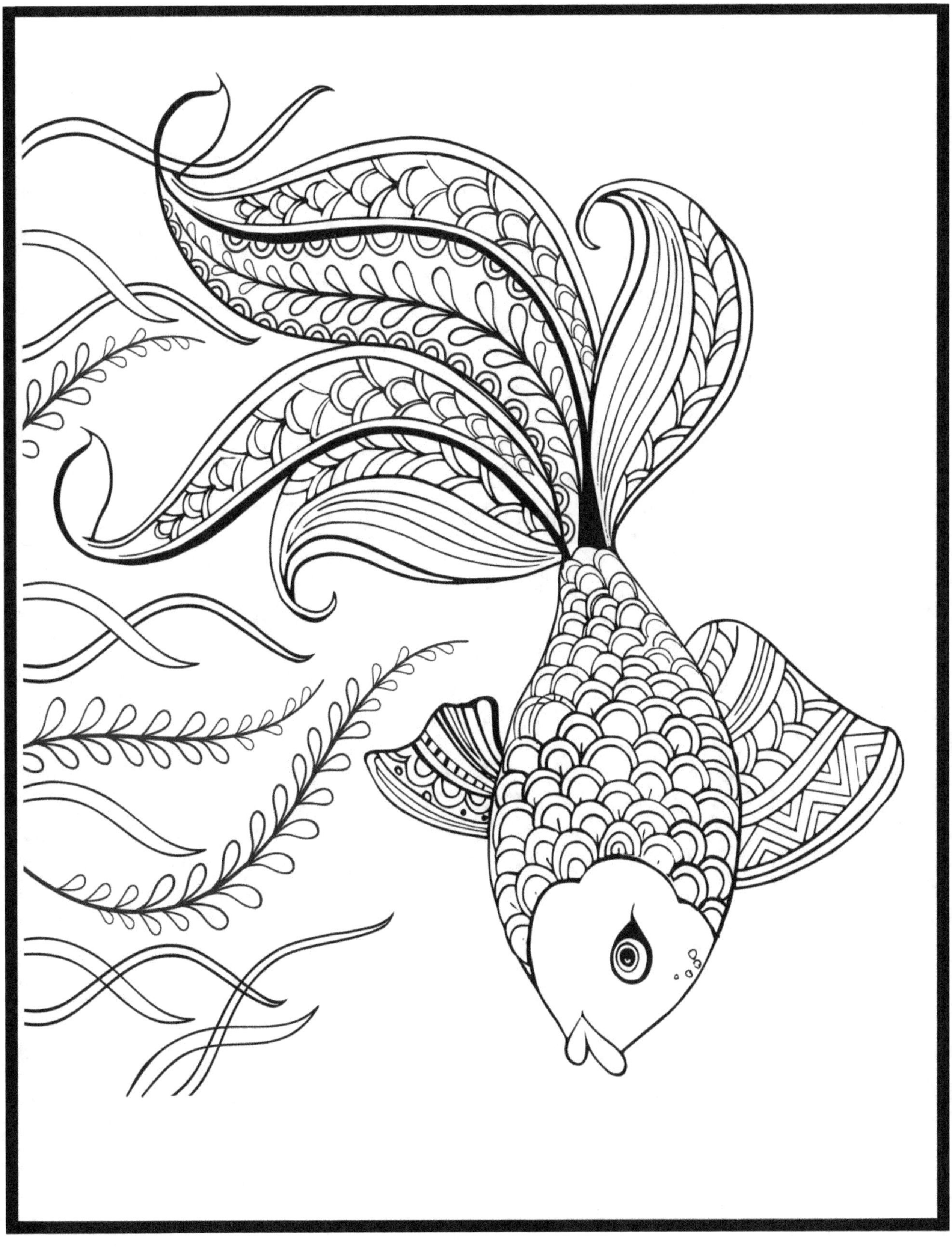

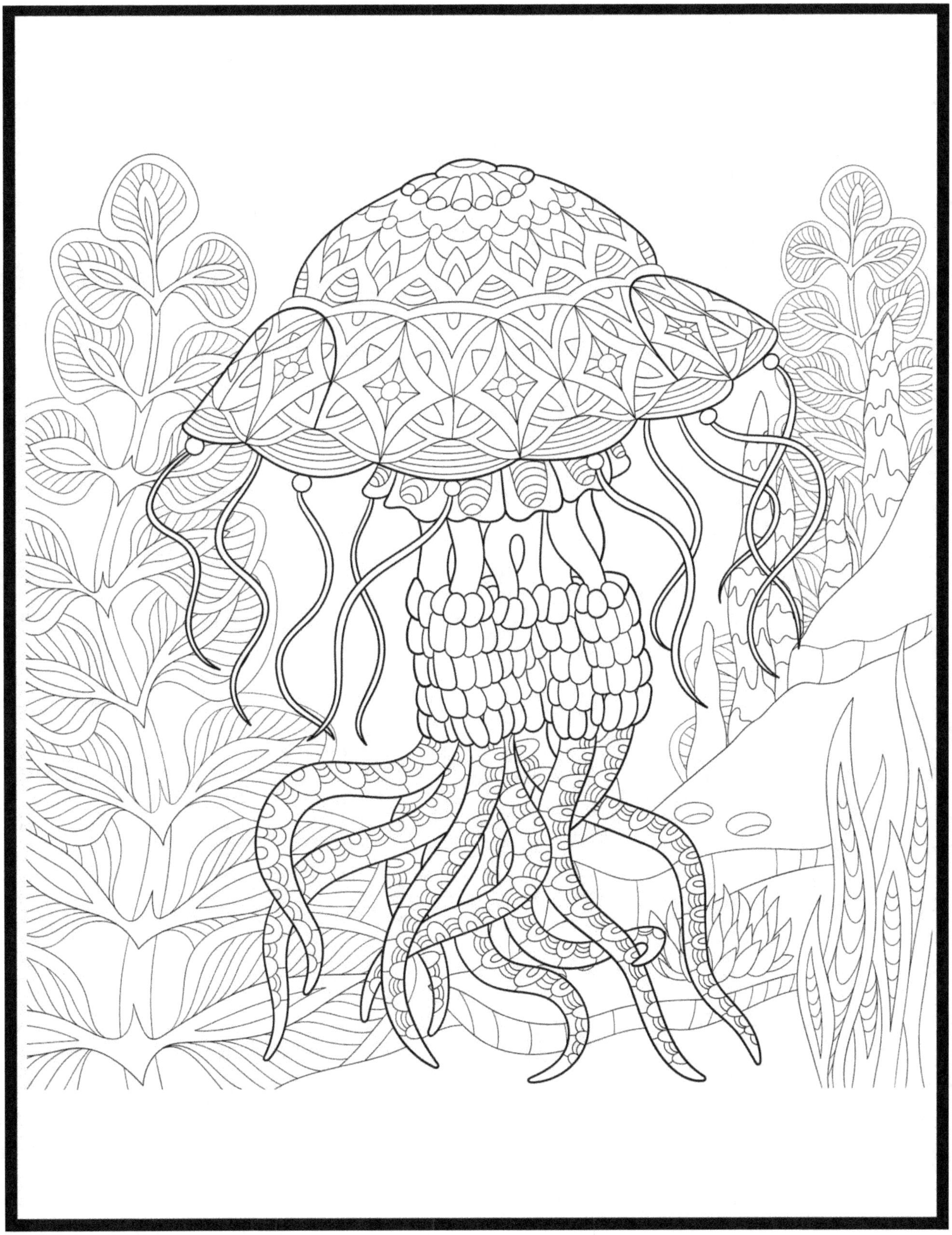

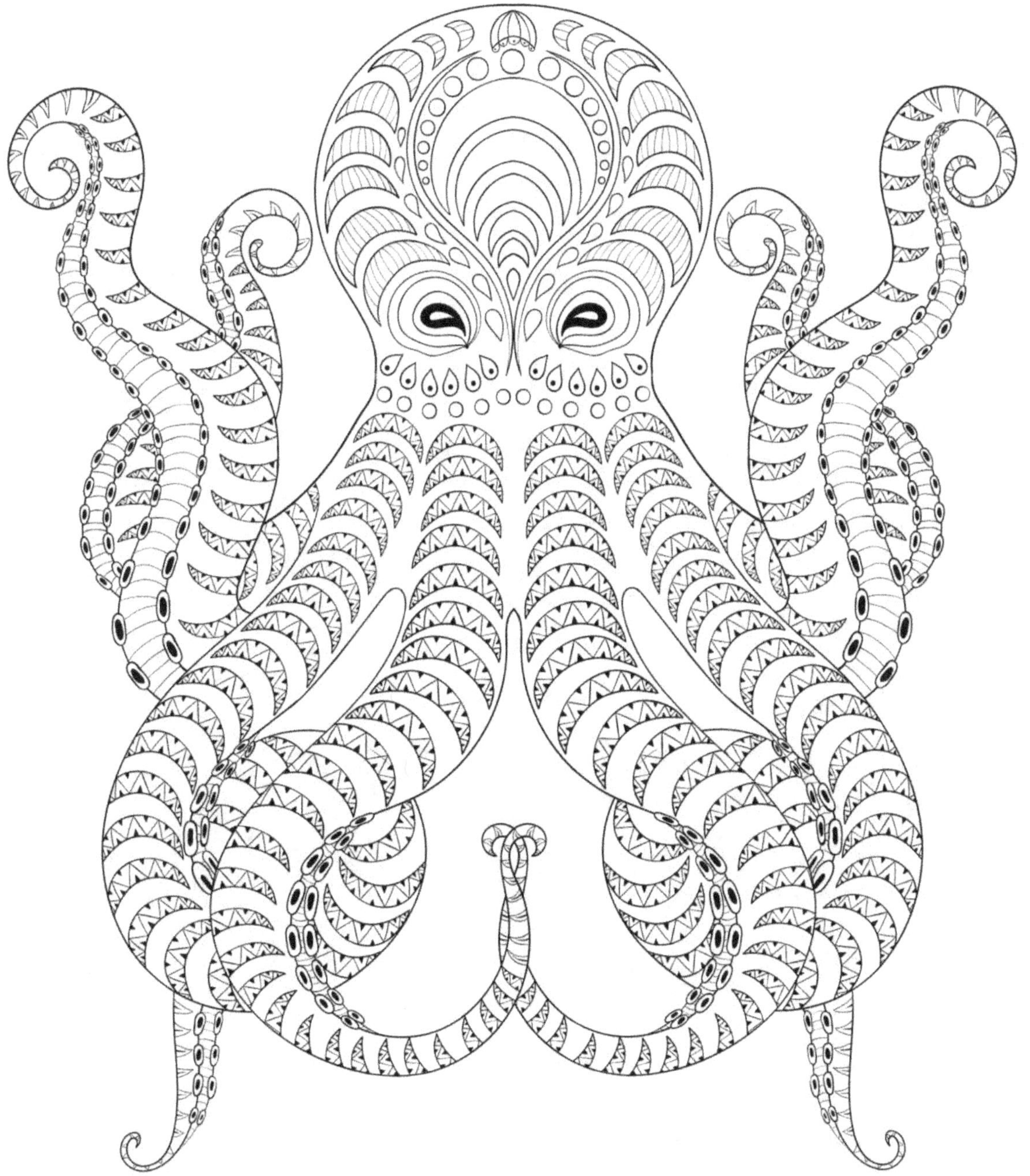

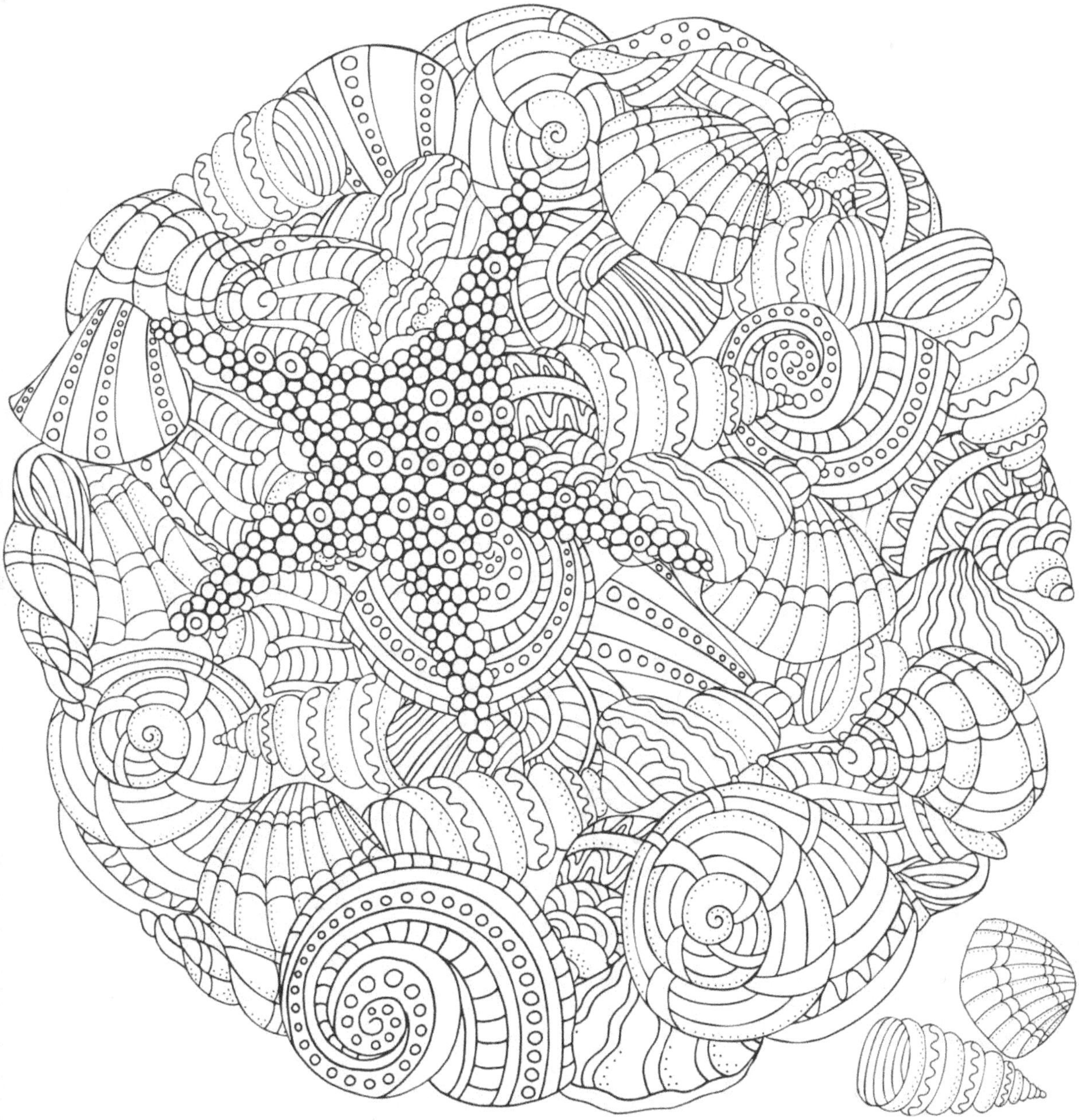

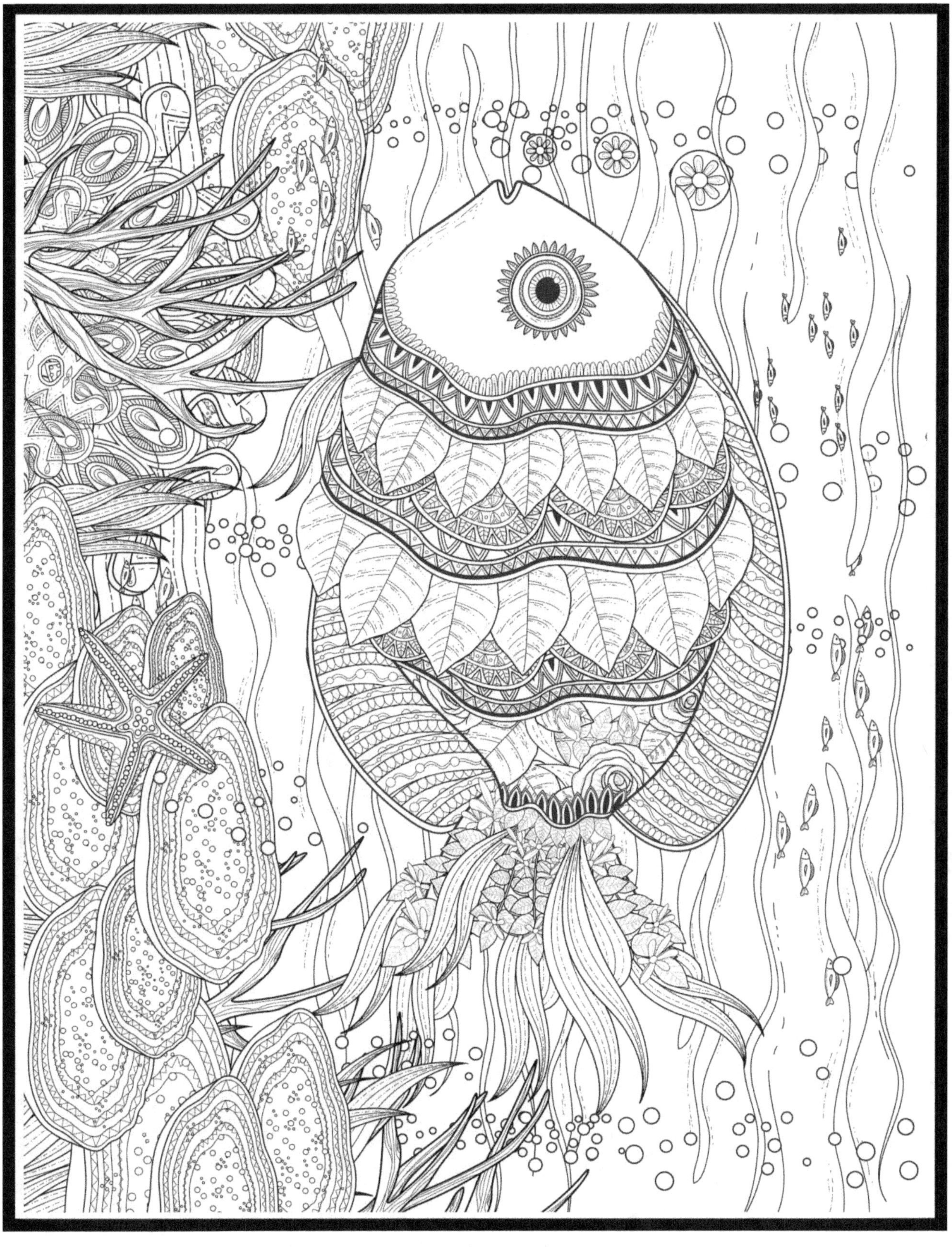

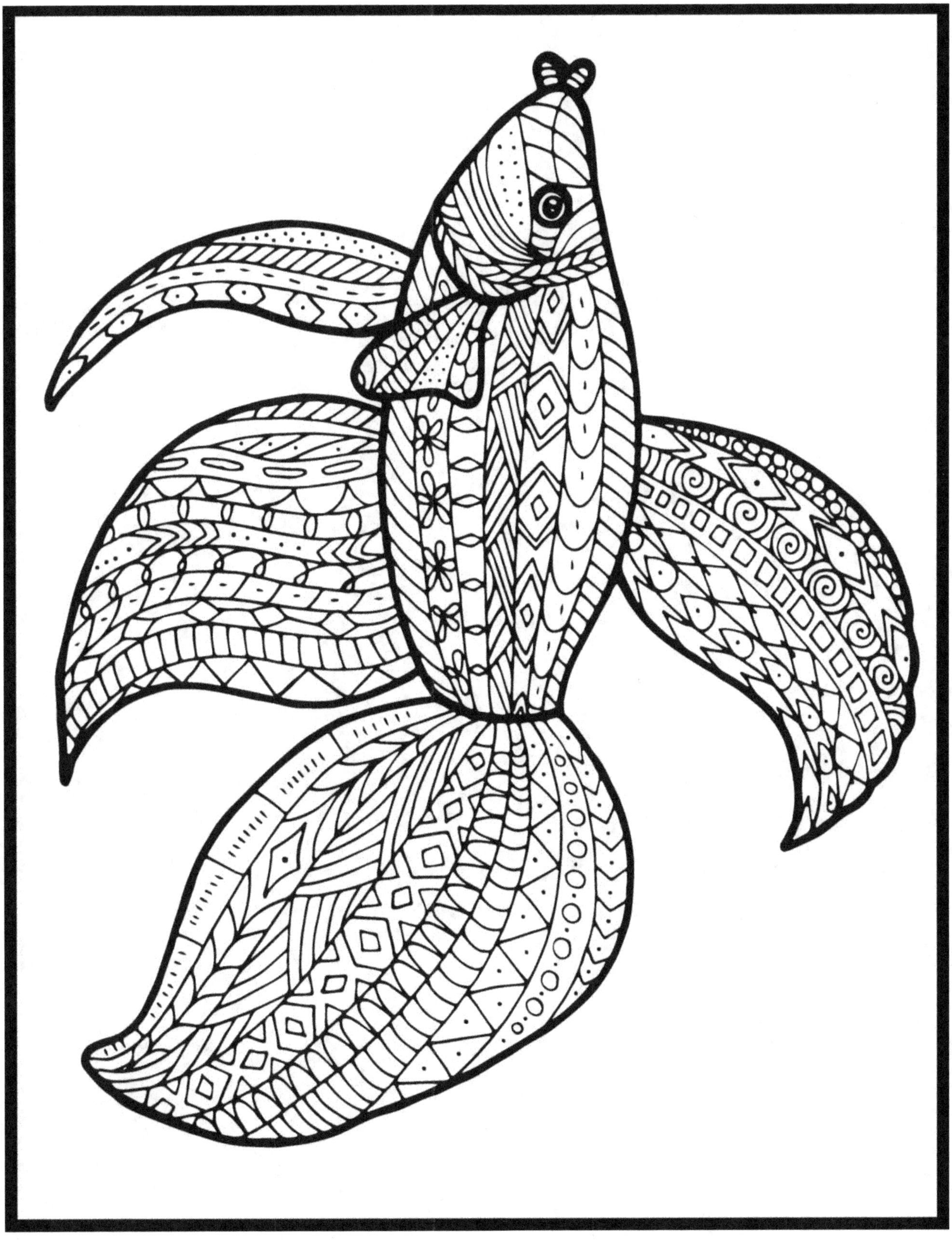

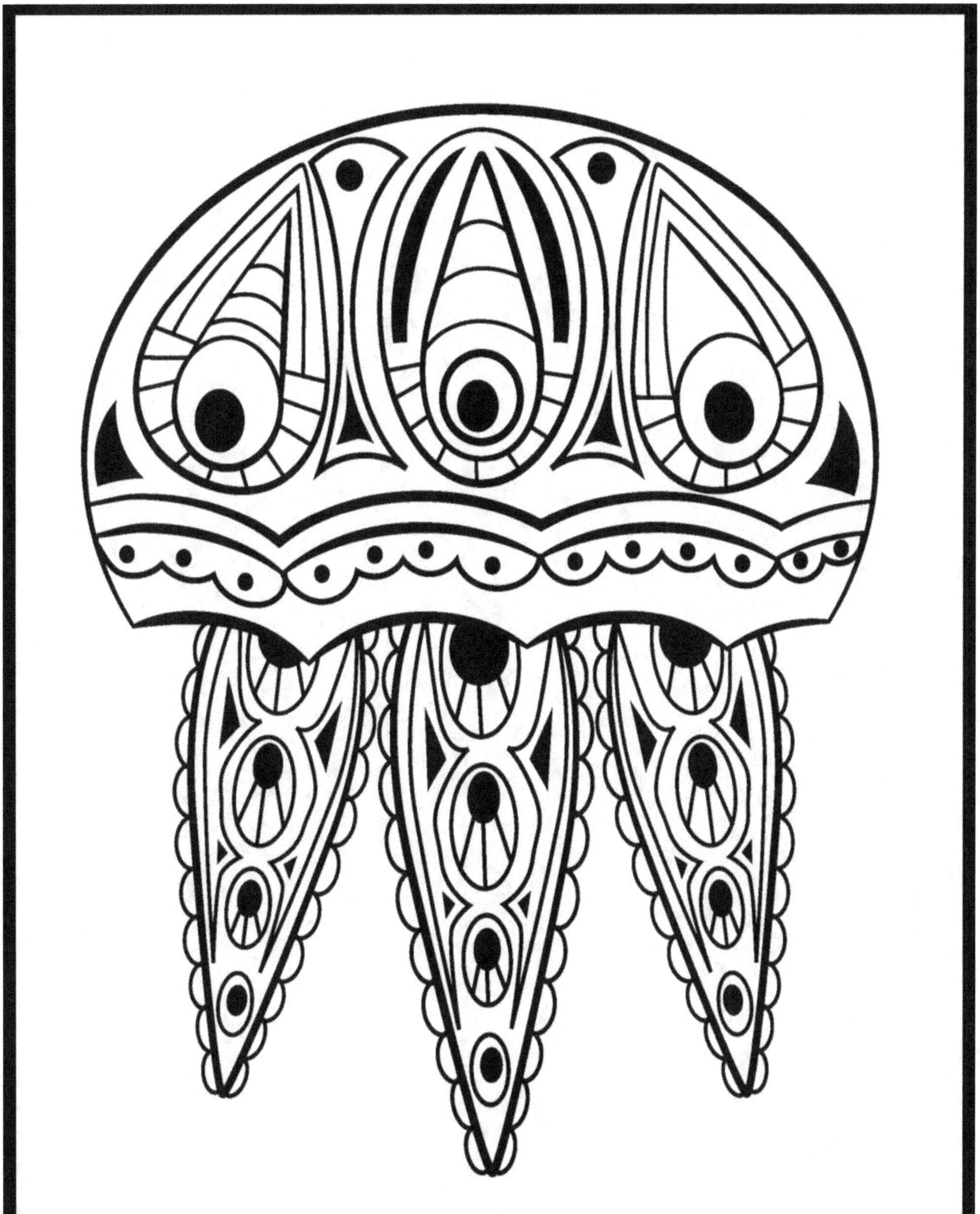

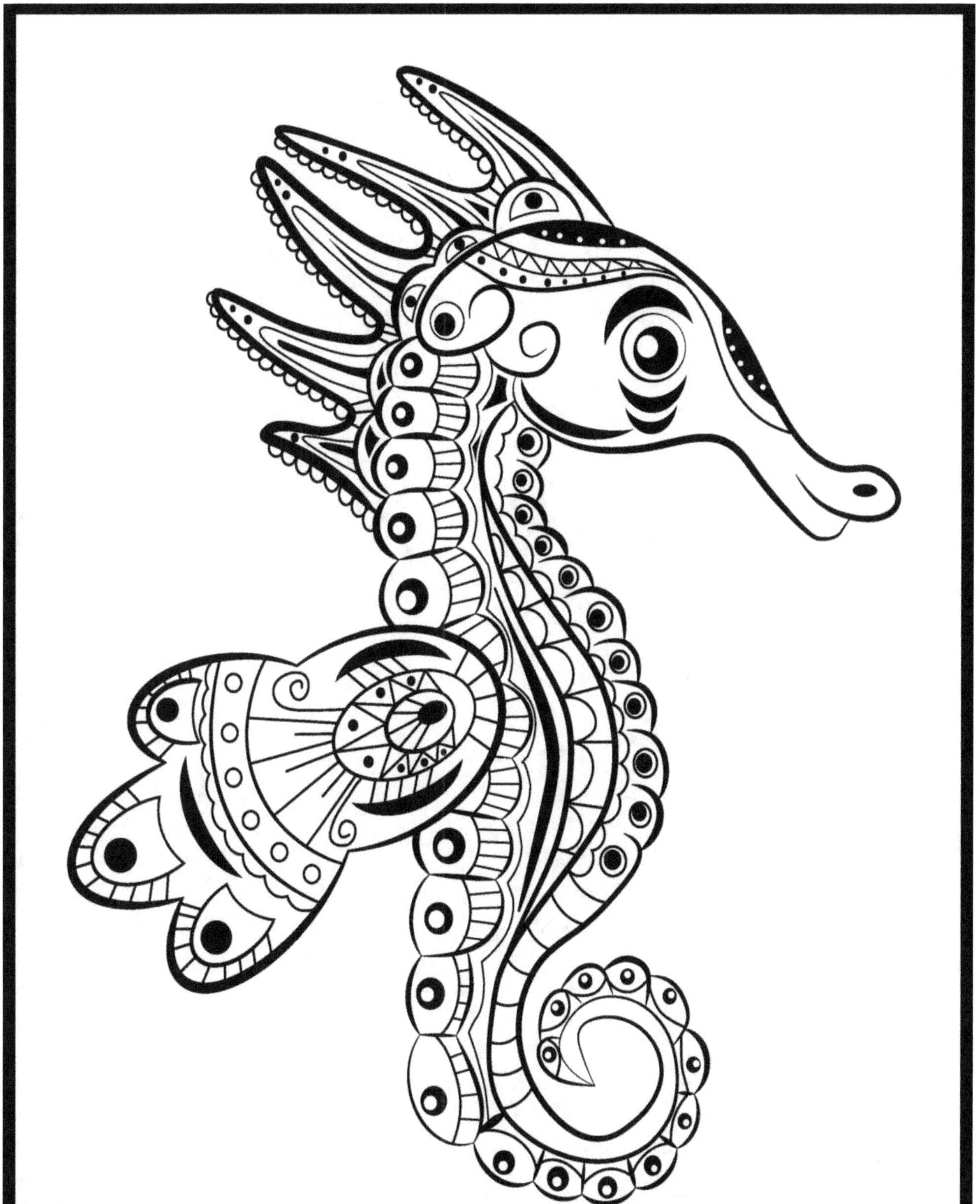

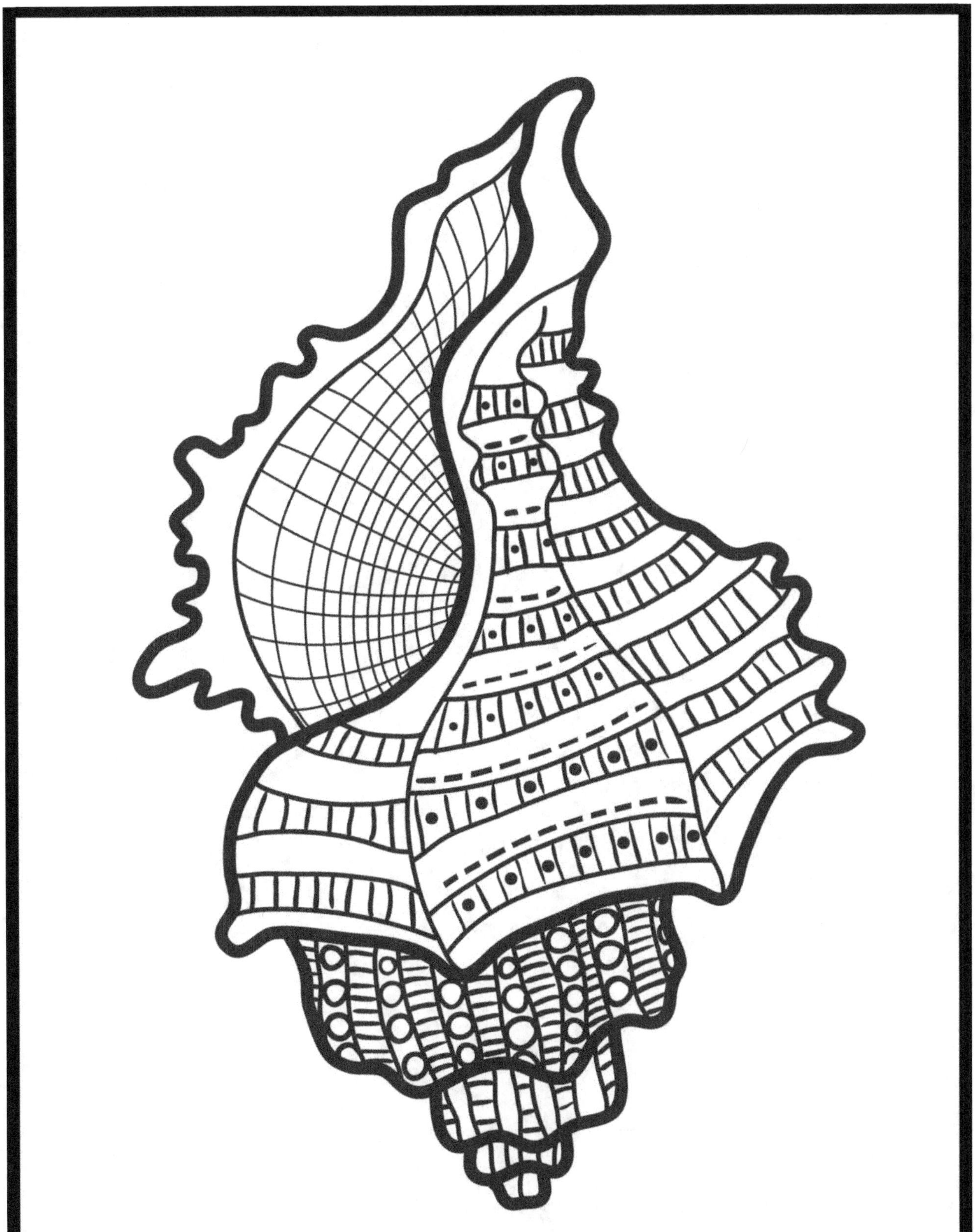

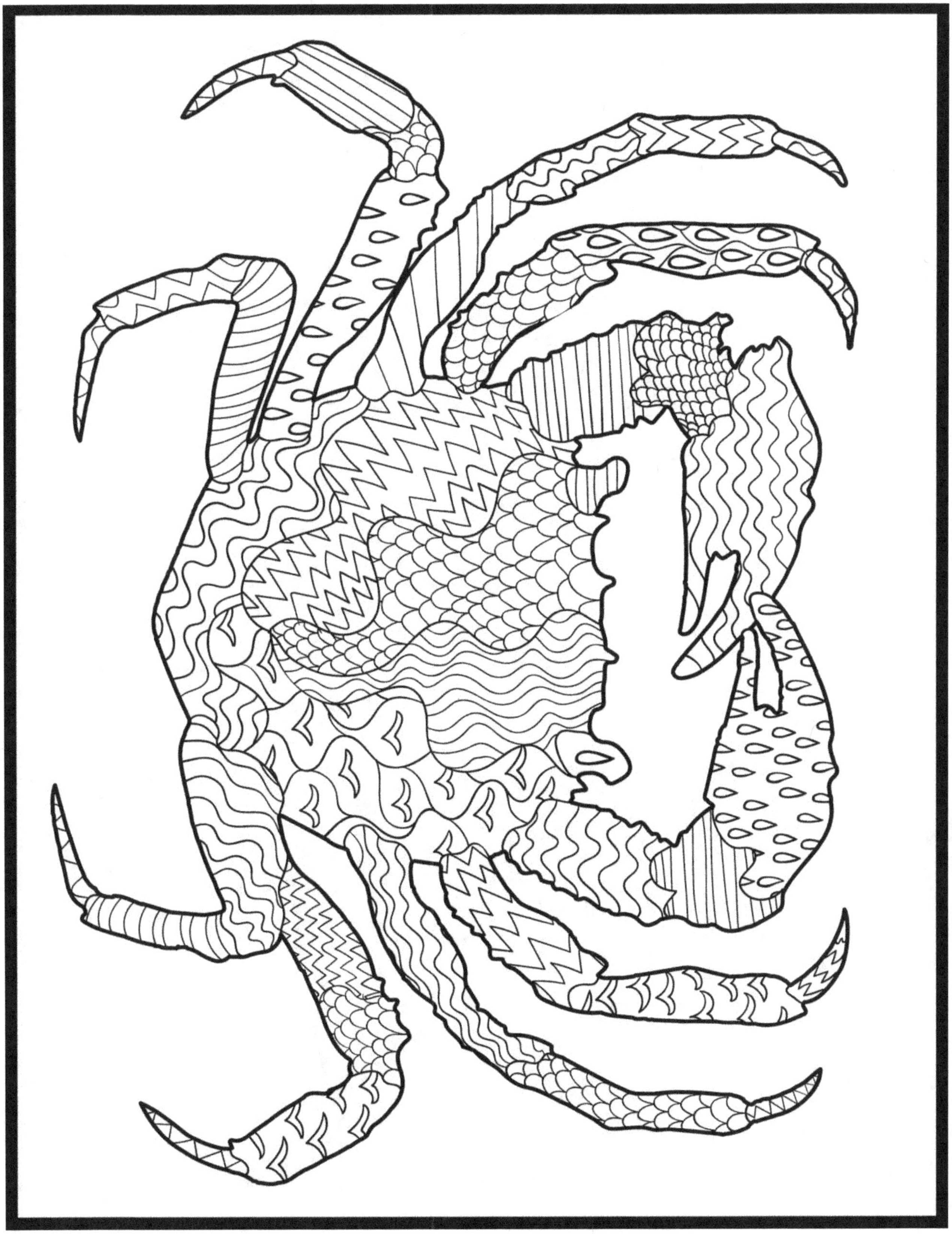

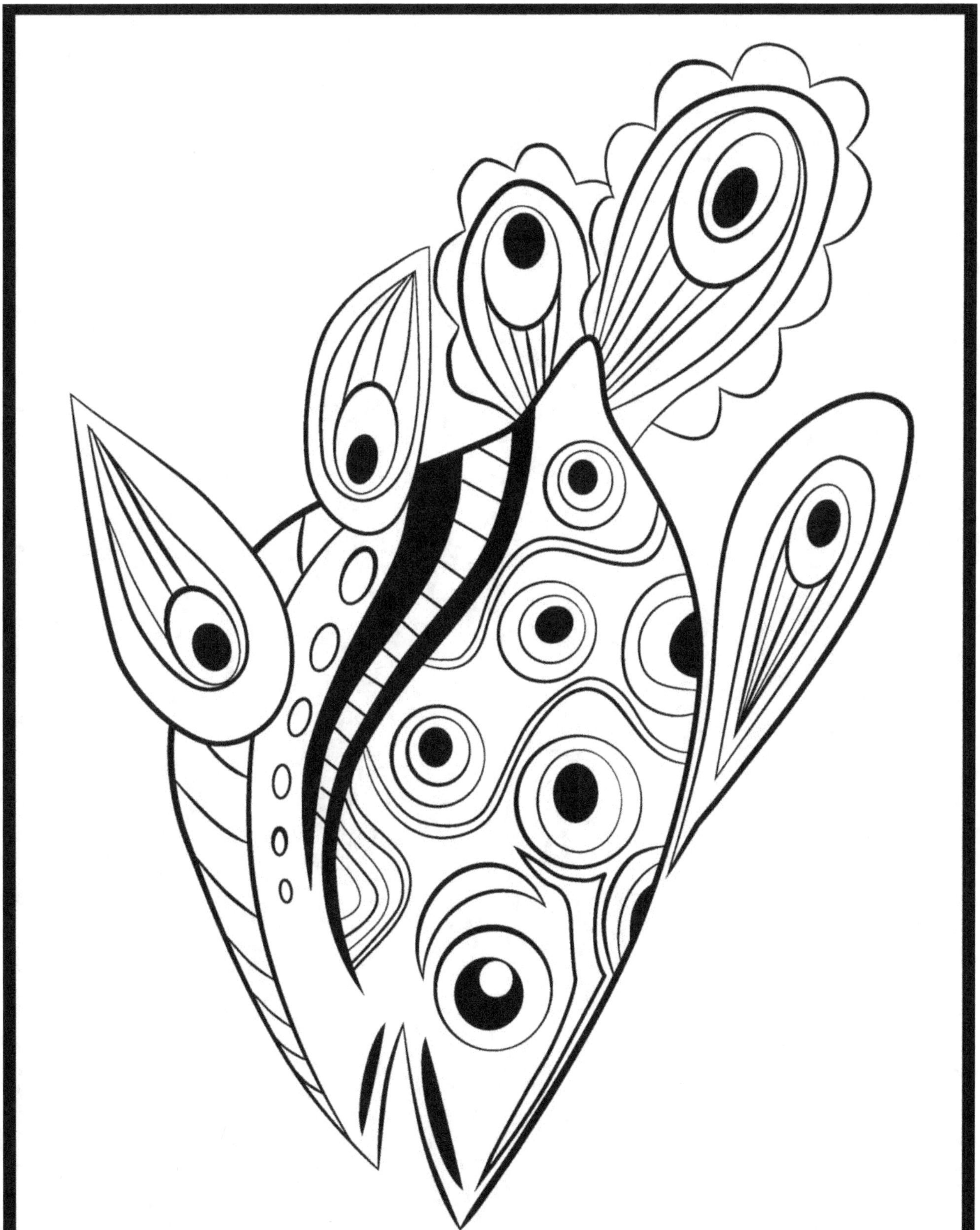

www.ingramcontent.com/pod-product-compliance
Lightning Source LLC
Chambersburg PA
CBHW082116220526
45472CB00009B/2200
9781720300083